Learning Advanced SQL

Wellesley Software

PRENTICE HALL, Englewood Cliffs, NJ 07632

Library of Congress Cataloging-in-Publication Data

Learning advanced SQL / Wellesley Software.
p. cm.
Includes index.
ISBN 0-13-528712-X
1. SQL (Computer program language) I. Wellesley Software (Firm)
QA76.73.S67L39 1992
005.75'6--dc20 91-26834
CIP

Acquisitions editor: Tom McElwee
Production editor: Joe Scordato
Prepress buyer: Linda Behrens
Manufacturing buyer: Dave Dickey

The author and publisher of this book have used their best efforts in preparing this book. These efforts include the development, research, and testing of the theories and programs to determine their effectiveness. The author and publisher make no warranty of any kind, expressed or implied, with regard to these programs or the documentation contained in this book. The author and publisher shall not be liable in any event for incidental or consequential damages in connection with, or arising out of, the furnishing, performance, or use of these programs.

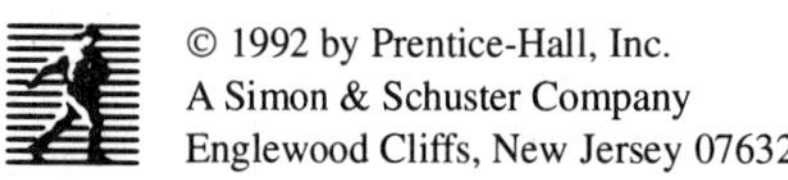

A Simon & Schuster Company
Englewood Cliffs, New Jersey 07632

Printed in the United States of America

10 9 8 7 6 5 4 3 2 1

ISBN 0-13-528712-X

Prentice-Hall International (UK) Limited, *London*
Prentice-Hall of Australia Pty. Limited, *Sydney*
Prentice-Hall Canada Inc., *Toronto*
Prentice-Hall Hispanoamericana, S.A., *Mexico*
Prentice-Hall of India Private Limited, *New Delhi*
Prentice-Hall of Japan, Inc., *Tokyo*
Simon & Schuster Asia Pte. Ltd., *Singapore*
Editora Prentice-Hall do Brasil, Ltda., *Rio de Janeiro*

Contents

PREFACE vii

1 INTRODUCTION AND REVIEW OF THE SELECT COMMAND 1

Basic Concepts of SQL 2
Practical Advantages 3
Sample Tables 4
Review of the SELECT Clause 5
Retrieving the Entire Table 7

2 ADVANCED CALCULATIONS 9

Review of Value Operators 9
Expressions with Several Operators 10
Expressions in the WHERE Clause 13
Expressions in the ORDER BY Clause 14
Workshop Exercises 16
Solutions to Workshop Exercises 21

3 ADVANCED USE OF AGGREGATE FUNCTIONS 25

Reviewing GROUP BY and HAVING 25
Summary Tables 28
Percentage of Total 29

Index Usage 31
Outer Join Techniques 32
Workshop Exercises 35
Solutions to Workshop Exercises 44

4 ADVANCED SUBQUERIES **53**

Complex Queries 53
Subqueries 57
ANY and ALL 62
Correlated Subqueries 63
EXISTS and NOT EXISTS 66
Workshop Exercises 68
Solutions to Workshop Exercises 74

5 ADVANCED USE OF JOINS **79**

Join Review 79
Substituting Joins for Subqueries 81
Joins with Control Tables 89
Joins with Subqueries 91
UNION 92
Views with Joins 95
Workshop Exercises 97
Solutions to Workshop Exercises 108

6 INTRODUCTION TO TRANSACTION CONTROLS **117**

Transactions 117
COMMIT 118
AUTOCOMMIT 119
ROLLBACK 120
Interaction of COMMIT, AUTOCOMMIT, ROLLBACK 120
Workshop Exercises 126
Solutions to Workshop Exercises 136

7 TABLES **141**

Review of Defining Tables 141
CREATE TABLE AS SELECT 144
DESCRIBE 146

Using Dictionary Tables to Review Work 147
COMMENT ON 150
ALTER TABLE 152
Workshop Exercises 154
Solutions to Workshop Exercises 163

8 VIEWS **169**

Review of Views 169
Views with Complex Queries 172
Modifying Data Through Views 174
Using Views to Enhance Security 178
Using Dictionary Tables to Examine Views 179
Workshop Exercises 182
Solutions to Workshop Exercises 191

APPENDICES **199**

A Sample Tables 199
B Quick Syntax Reference 201
C Glossary 207

INDEX **211**

Preface

THE NEED FOR THIS TEXT

SQL (Structured Query Language) has rapidly become the worldwide standard for relational database manipulation and control. It is now included with every major relational database management system on the market today.

SQL was developed in the late 1970s by IBM® as part of a research project on relational databases. Since then IBM has carefully orchestrated a strategy for SQL that has propelled this language to the forefront of executive MIS decisions.

Despite the emergence of SQL as a standard, there exists little coverage of this language. Vendors provide sparse coverage in their product documentation, and even texts devoted to database management include only a few chapters on this important language. A need exists for a text dedicated to providing a thorough understanding of SQL in a practical manner. It should begin with the concepts and syntax usage, but provide numerous examples to illustrate the implementation. Furthermore, it should challenge students through a series of workshop exercises that reinforce the concepts they have just learned. Finally, it should provide students an opportunity to try these new skills on a computer, in a simulated SQL environment. Individually these three approaches to learning are barely satisfactory. But together they would provide the most comprehensive text available today to learn SQL. This text does all this.

AUDIENCE

The intended audience for Learning Advanced SQL is individuals who want to gain a working knowledge of the advanced features of SQL in the most efficient way possible. In a college or university setting the course may be used as an ideal supplement to a principles of databases course or any course dealing with relational database management systems.

A basic familiarity with relational databases and SQL is assumed. This can be achieved by using the precursor to this text, *Learning SQL.*

OBJECTIVES

Upon completion of this text the student should be able to make more extensive use of the SELECT command, perform advanced calculations, use advanced aggregate functions, perform advanced subqueries and joins, control transactions, and make more extensive use of views and indexes.

COVERAGE

Topics covered in this text include an introduction to SQL, the query language, data manipulation language, data definition language, and transaction controls. Although SQL has become an international standard for relational database languages, some vendors offer extensions to SQL that are particular to their products. This text attempts to cover the advanced features and applications of standard SQL, but in some cases useful nonstandard features must also be explained. Occasionally this text will examine advanced features of the ORACLE RDBMS.

HOW TO USE THIS TEXT

This text has been carefully designed to provide the maximum learning through presentation of the topic material, examples, case study workshop exercises, and computer-based exercises.

Students should always begin with the topic presentation section. This section is named by chapter (Chapter 1, Chapter 2, and so on). Each chapter is immediately followed by a Workshop Exercises section. This section provides reinforcement of the topics presented through paper-based exercises. The solutions are provided at the end of each chapter.

Once students have completed the topic presentation (chapter) and the Workshop Exercises, they should next go to the computer-based exercises to hone their new-found skills.

Once students have taken all three components, they should move on to the next topic (chapter).

The text was designed to be taken in this order. You will receive the maximum benefit of this text by adhering to this plan.

APPENDICES

Appendices at the end of the text include the Sample Tables, a Quick Syntax Reference, and a Glossary.

ACKNOWLEDGMENTS

Major contributors to this text include Daniel D. McFadden, David B. Rubinstein, and Joseph E. Gustafson.

1

Introduction and Review of the SELECT Command

Structured Query Language (SQL) is a fourth-generation language developed by IBM® research over a period of many years. Although IBM developed SQL, it has become an international standard for database languages and is now provided by a majority of the prominent database vendors in their product offerings.

SQL is an English-like language used for accessing and controlling a database. End users with little or no data processing experience can quickly learn the basic features of SQL, yet data processing professionals will find that SQL provides a set of powerful and complete facilities which they require. Therefore, SQL becomes the common language between end users and data processing professionals alike!

SQL is intended to be used by a variety of different audiences:

- End Users
- Data Processing Professionals
- Applications Developers
- Database Administrators
- Management
- Information Center Staff
- And many more

With SQL, all data are accessed via a standard user interface. Therefore, SQL provides an opportunity for all your computers and users to speak the same language. SQL will reduce the amount of training required by employees as they move from different departments and systems.

SQL is many times more productive than traditional programming languages such as COBOL. With SQL, a program can be written in several lines of code, compared to several pages when using traditional programming languages. Therefore, development costs are only a fraction of the costs incurred with these traditional languages.

SQL is the standard relational database language, now used in every major computing environment. It can be used interactively from a terminal, or if needed, it can be embedded in standard programming languages such as COBOL, Fortran, PL/I, Pascal, C, and ADA.

Embedding SQL in these languages allows you complete flexibility in building applications.

SQL provides a single, comprehensive language for:

- Query — retrieving data from the database
- Data Manipulation — inserting, updating, and deleting data in the database
- Data Definition — adding new tables, views, and indexes to the database
- Data Control — preventing access to private data in the database

SQL can be used as the standard vehicle for accessing data across a wide variety of hardware and operating environments. These environments range from personal computers to minicomputers and mainframes.

BASIC CONCEPTS OF SQL

When using SQL, information is stored in relational databases. Simply stated, a relational database is a collection of tables. In a table, data are arranged in two dimensions, vertical columns and horizontal rows.

For example, the department table listed below has three (3) columns and four (4) rows.

```
DEPT

     DEPTNO DNAME          LOC
 ========== ========== ==========
         10 ACCOUNTING NEW YORK
         20 RESEARCH   DALLAS
         30 SALES      CHICAGO
         40 OPERATIONS BOSTON
```

SQL tables are two dimensional having a specified number of columns, and a variable number of unordered rows.

A row is an entry in the table. Each row is characterized by a number of attributes called *columns*. For example, each row in the department table (DEPT) is characterized by a department number (DEPTNO), a department name (DNAME), and a location (LOC).

The intersection of a column and a row is called a *value*. Each value is one of the available data types, or null. In the above table, SALES is an example of a value.

PRACTICAL ADVANTAGES

There are many practical advantages to using the relational model for databases. A relational database is easy to learn because there is only one simple data structure, namely, the table. As a result, it is conceptually easy for a user to select, manipulate, and control data using SQL.

Using SQL, the operator simply states the results desired, rather than defining a procedure to derive the results. The user specifies the operations in terms of *what* is to be done, *not how* to do it. In other words, SQL and relational databases are *nonprocedural.*

Because SQL and relational databases are nonprocedural, there is no need to predefine access paths for the database. The SQL system will automatically find a path to the records you want without any intervention whatsoever from the user. This concept is called *automatic navigation* and is one of the major reasons why SQL and relational databases increase programmer productivity and can easily be used by the novice.

With SQL, data are readily accessible to all classes of users. Relational database management systems provide a query optimizer that will automatically search for the most efficient path to retrieve the desired result. This optimizer automatically adapts to the table structure or schema without requiring that you modify your applications.

Another major reason why relational databases are so productive is that their schema can be modified on-line without disruption of existing applications. New columns and tables can be added at any time without the worry of changing existing programs or predefined navigation paths.

SAMPLE TABLES

EMP

EMPNO	ENAME	JOB	MGR	HIREDATE	SAL	COMM	DEPTNO
7369	SMITH	CLERK	7902	17-DEC-1980	800		20
7499	ALLEN	SALESMAN	7698	20-FEB-1981	1600	300	30
7521	WARD	SALESMAN	7698	22-FEB-1981	1250	500	30
7566	JONES	MANAGER	7839	02-APR-1981	2975		20
7654	MARTIN	SALESMAN	7698	28-SEP-1981	1250	1400	30
7698	BLAKE	MANAGER	7839	01-MAY-1981	2850		30
7782	CLARK	MANAGER	7839	09-JUN-1981	2450		10
7788	SCOTT	ANALYST	7566	09-DEC-1982	3000		20
7839	KING	PRESIDENT		17-NOV-1981	5000		10
7844	TURNER	SALESMAN	7698	08-SEP-1981	1500	0	30
7876	ADAMS	CLERK	7788	12-JAN-1983	1100		20
7900	JAMES	CLERK	7698	03-DEC-1981	950		30
7902	FORD	ANALYST	7566	03-DEC-1981	3000		20
7934	MILLER	CLERK	7782	23-JAN-1982	1300		10

DEPT

DEPTNO	DNAME	LOC
10	ACCOUNTING	NEW YORK
20	RESEARCH	DALLAS
30	SALES	CHICAGO
40	OPERATIONS	BOSTON

BONUS

ENAME	JOB	SAL	COMM
SMITH	CLERK	800	
ALLEN	SALESMAN	1600	300
WARD	SALESMAN	1250	500
JONES	MANAGER	2975	
MARTIN	SALESMAN	1250	1400

SALGRADE

GRADE	LOSAL	HISAL
1	700	1200
2	1201	1400
3	1401	2000
4	2001	3000
5	3001	9999

These are the tables we will use to demonstrate the features and capabilities of SQL. If needed, a template of each table will be provided later in the text or in the on-disk exercises.

REVIEW OF THE SELECT CLAUSE

Let's review the syntax of the basic SQL SELECT statement used to retrieve data from a table. The basic SELECT statement consists of two clauses, the SELECT clause and the FROM clause:

```
SELECT <column_name(s) / *>
FROM <table_name>;
```

The SELECT clause tells the relational database management system (RDBMS) which columns should be retrieved from the table specified in the FROM clause.

The asterisk (*) can be used as a wildcard to indicate that all columns should be retrieved from the table.

Typically, you specify in the SELECT clause the column names defined in the CREATE TABLE statement or the ALTER TABLE statement. (CREATE

TABLE specifies the design of a new table. ALTER TABLE designates a column or columns to add to an existing table.)

This is the EMP table, an example of a typical user table.

EMPNO	ENAME	JOB	MGR	HIREDATE	SAL	COMM	DEPTNO
7369	SMITH	CLERK	7902	17-DEC-80	800		20
7499	ALLEN	SALESMAN	7698	20-FEB-81	1600	300	30
7521	WARD	SALESMAN	7698	22-FEB-81	1250	500	30
7566	JONES	MANAGER	7839	02-APR-81	2975		20
7654	MARTIN	SALESMAN	7698	28-SEP-81	1250	1400	30
7698	BLAKE	MANAGER	7839	01-MAY-81	2850		30
7782	CLARK	MANAGER	7839	09-JUN-81	2450		10
7788	SCOTT	ANALYST	7566	09-DEC-82	3000		20
7839	KING	PRESIDENT		17-NOV-81	5000		10
7844	TURNER	SALESMAN	7698	08-SEP-81	1500	0	30
7876	ADAMS	CLERK	7788	12-JAN-83	1100		20
7900	JAMES	CLERK	7698	03-DEC-81	950		30
7902	FORD	ANALYST	7566	03-DEC-81	3000		20
7934	MILLER	CLERK	7782	23-JAN-82	1300		10

Retrieving data from the database is the most common SQL operation. A database retrieval is called a *query*. To issue a query you use the SELECT command, which has two parts, called clauses.

```
SELECT  column-name, list of column-names, or *
FROM    table-name, or list of table-names;
```

The SELECT clause is always entered first and is immediately followed by the FROM clause. You must specify the exact column names and table names in the query.

The most simple case when using SQL is to list the entire contents of a table. This can be easily accomplished by issuing the following SQL query:

```
SELECT  *
FROM    table-name;
```

The asterisk (or column names if listed) and table names are not keywords but rather tell the system what information is to be retrieved. In this case, the * indicates that all columns should be displayed in the result.

RETRIEVING THE ENTIRE TABLE

Example

If we would like to display all the contents of the table named EMPLOYEE, the correct SQL syntax would be:

```
SELECT  *
FROM    EMP;
```

RESULT:

EMP

EMPNO	ENAME	JOB	MGR	HIREDATE	SAL	COMM	DEPTNO
7369	SMITH	CLERK	7902	17-DEC-1980	800		20
7499	ALLEN	SALESMAN	7698	20-FEB-1981	1600	300	30
7521	WARD	SALESMAN	7698	22-FEB-1981	1250	500	30
7566	JONES	MANAGER	7839	02-APR-1981	2975		20
7654	MARTIN	SALESMAN	7698	28-SEP-1981	1250	1400	30
7698	BLAKE	MANAGER	7839	01-MAY-1981	2850		30
7782	CLARK	MANAGER	7839	09-JUN-1981	2450		10
7788	SCOTT	ANALYST	7566	09-DEC-1982	3000		20
7839	KING	PRESIDENT		17-NOV-1981	5000		10
7844	TURNER	SALESMAN	7698	08-SEP-1981	1500	0	30
7876	ADAMS	CLERK	7788	12-JAN-1983	1100		20
7900	JAMES	CLERK	7698	03-DEC-1981	950		30
7902	FORD	ANALYST	7566	03-DEC-1981	3000		20
7934	MILLER	CLERK	7782	23-JAN-1982	1300		10

Once again, notice the semicolon at the end of the query. It is used as a statement terminator. The semicolon (;) statement terminator functions like the English sentence terminator, the period (.). A sentence in English needs to be terminated (ended) with a period (.) and every SQL statement must be ended with the statement terminator, a semicolon (;).

In this past example SQL has displayed all the information in the EMP table exactly as it is stored in the database.

The remaining chapters in this book will help you sharpen your existing SQL skills and build upon those skills with advanced topics.

2

Advanced Calculations

REVIEW OF VALUE OPERATORS

This lesson examines calculations in SQL. The following operators are used in SQL calculations:

+	Addition
-	Subtraction
*	Multiplication
/	Division

You perform a calculation in SQL by including an arithmetic expression in an SQL command. An arithmetic expression consists of the names of columns containing numeric values and numbers connected by the value operators +, -, *, and /.

To display the result of a calculation, include an arithmetic expression in a SELECT clause, as you would a column name.

Here is an example of the use of a calculation (arithmetic expression) in a SELECT statement.

Example

Suppose that clerks have 25% of their salary withheld for income tax. You can calculate the amount to be withheld by including the arithmetic expression SAL * .25 in a SELECT clause querying the EMP table:

```
SELECT SAL, SAL * .25
FROM EMP
WHERE JOB = 'CLERK';
```

This results in:

```
    SAL  SAL*.25
------- -------
    800      200
   1100      275
    950    237.5
   1300      325
```

The RDBMS automatically chooses the expression SAL*.25 as the column heading for the column containing the results of the calculation.

EXPRESSIONS WITH SEVERAL OPERATORS

You can use more than one value operator (+, -, *, /) in an arithmetic expression.

For example, at the end of the year, you need to calculate the salaries of salespeople for income tax purposes. Because the salary amounts in the EMP table are monthly amounts, the total income for a salesperson is the SAL value multiplied by 12. Then you need to add to the salary the commission (COMM) value. A COMM value is not multiplied by 12, because it represents commission to date.

Example

Here is the query you use to calculate the total incomes of salespeople:

```
SELECT ENAME, SAL * 12 + COMM
FROM EMP
WHERE JOB = 'SALESMAN';
```

Here is the table that results. Note that the expression SAL * 12 + COMM, representing total income, is used automatically as the column heading for the results of this calculation.

```
ENAME          SAL*12+COMM
----------     -----------
ALLEN                19500
WARD                 15500
MARTIN               16400
TURNER               18000
```

The expression in the previous query, SAL * 12 + COMM, was executed left to right. But are all expressions executed from left to right? And are addition, subtraction, multiplication, and division given the same precedence?

Not all expressions are executed from left to right, because of the operator precedence of the +, -, *, and / value operators.

As in traditional arithmetic, all multiplication and division operations are executed first. Then the addition and subtraction operations are executed, from left to right.

Any multiplication and division operations that are next to each other are executed from left to right. Any addition and subtraction operations that are next to each other are executed from left to right.

The multiplication and division operations have equal precedence. The addition and subtraction have equal, lower precedence, occurring after multiplication and division operations.

What impact does the value operator precedence have on calculations? Here is another example involving the salespeople in the company represented by the EMP table.

Example

Suppose you want to calculate the average monthly income for each salesperson. To do this, you could divide the total income, as calculated in our previous example, by 12. Your query might be:

```
SELECT ENAME, SAL * 12 + COMM / 12
FROM EMP
WHERE JOB = 'SALESMAN';
```

The result:

```
ENAME           SAL*12+COMM/12
----------      --------------
ALLEN                    19225
WARD                   15041.7
MARTIN                 15116.7
TURNER                   18000
```

The expression SAL * 12 + COMM / 12 represents the average monthly income. Or does it? Remember, multiplications and divisions take precedence over additions and subtractions and are executed first. Therefore, SAL * 12 is calculated, and COMM / 12 is calculated, and the results of these two calculations are added to give the result.

This is not correct.

To find the average monthly salary, SAL * 12 must be calculated, then added to COMM, and the resulting number must be divided by 12.

Here is an instance where the rules of precedence (multiplication and division first, followed by addition and subtraction) need to be overridden.

You can override the normal precedence of the value operators (+, -, *, /) by enclosing an arithmetic expression (calculation) in parentheses. Because the expression SAL * 12 + COMM should be evaluated before it is divided by 12, enclose it in parentheses:

```
SELECT ENAME, (SAL * 12 + COMM) / 12
FROM EMP
WHERE JOB = 'SALESMAN';
```

Enclosing SAL * 12 + COMM in parentheses ensures that the expression is evaluated before the division by 12 is performed.

Here is the correct solution to the problem. The column with the heading (SAL*12+COMM)/12 contains the average monthly salary for salespeople.

```
ENAME          (SAL*12+COMM)/12
----------     ----------------
ALLEN                      1625
WARD                    1291.67
MARTIN                  1366.67
TURNER                     1500
```

EXPRESSIONS IN THE WHERE CLAUSE

When a calculation is included in a SELECT clause, the results of the calculation are displayed as if the calculation is a column in a table.

However, the use of calculations is not limited to the SELECT clause. Arithmetic expressions may also be used in the WHERE clause of a query, in conjunction with logical operators.

The logical operators include:

= (equal to)
!=, ^=, < > (not equal to)
> (greater than)
>= (greater than or equal to)
< (less than)
<= (less than or equal to)

and

NOT.

Example

Suppose you want a list of those employees whose commission to date (COMM value) is less than 25% of their monthly salary (SAL value).

Here, you want to list only those employees with a COMM value less than (<) .25 * SAL. Use the calculation .25 * SAL in the WHERE clause of your query:

```
SELECT ENAME, SAL, COMM
FROM EMP
WHERE COMM < .25 * SAL;
```

Two employees, and their SAL and COMM values, are listed:

```
ENAME            SAL      COMM
----------   -------   -------
ALLEN           1600       300
TURNER          1500         0
```

EXPRESSIONS IN THE ORDER BY CLAUSE

You have seen that calculations (arithmetic expressions) can be used in both the SELECT and WHERE clauses. In ORACLE, you can also use calculations in the ORDER BY clause to sort the results of a query. Most other RDBMSs do not permit this, however.

Example

Suppose you want a list of the salespeople in the company. You want the list to include the salesperson's name, monthly salary, commission to date, and the difference between the monthly salary value and the the commission-to-date value. Finally, you want the result to be ordered by that difference.

Here is a query to use:

```
SELECT ENAME, SAL, COMM, SAL - COMM
FROM EMP
WHERE JOB = 'SALESMAN'
ORDER BY SAL - COMM;
```

Here is the result:

```
ENAME            SAL      COMM    SAL-COMM
----------   -------   -------    --------
MARTIN          1250      1400        -150
WARD            1250       500         750
ALLEN           1600       300        1300
TURNER          1500         0        1500
```

The result is ordered by the SAL-COMM values. Notice that the SAL-COMM value for MARTIN is a negative number. It is preceded by a negative sign (-) and listed first when the table is sorted in ascending order.

In this chapter, you learned how to:

- Use expressions with several value operators
- Identify expressions in the WHERE clause
- Employ expressions in the ORDER BY clause

Now let's try some exercises to reinforce these topics.

Workshop Exercises

Advanced Calculations

Welcome to the workshop exercises for this chapter. Let's try a few questions to improve your skills. In these exercises, you will practice the following concepts:

1. Simple numeric expression formats
2. The use of parentheses to override operator precedence
3. The use of expressions in the ORDER BY clause

Exercise 2.1

Let's review simple numeric expression formats. Show all MANAGERs by name from the EMP table along with each one's SAL figure and the four expressions defined below:

- Salary plus 100
- Salary minus 100
- Salary multiplied by 1.267
- Salary divided by -1.267

RESULT TABLE:

```
ENAME      SAL   SAL+100  SAL-100  SAL*1.267  SAL/-1.267
-----  -------   -------  -------  ---------  ----------
JONES     2975      3075     2875   3769.325     -2348.1
BLAKE     2850      2950     2750    3610.95     -2249.4
CLARK     2450      2550     2350    3104.15     -1933.7
```

Write your answer here:

____

____

____

____

____

____

Exercise 2.2

For Managers, show the ENAME, SAL, and the result of changing the salary as follows: Take 75% of the salary after first increasing it by 550.

RESULT TABLE:

```
ENAME            SAL   0.75 * (SAL + 550)
--------     -------   ------------------
JONES        2975.00              2643.75
BLAKE        2850.00              2550.00
CLARK        2450.00              2250.00
```

Write your answer here:

____

____

____

____

____

____

Exercise 2.3

Repeat Exercise 2.2, but now show only those rows of the results in which the "new" salary computes to be greater than 2500. (Hint: You'll need an expression in the WHERE clause.)

RESULT TABLE:

```
ENAME          SAL    0.75 * (SAL + 550)
--------   -------    ------------------
JONES      2975.00               2643.75
BLAKE      2850.00               2550.00
```

Write your answer here:

______

______

______

______

______

______

Exercise 2.4

Repeat Exercise 2.3, but this time sort the results by the "new" salary. Don't use its "position" number.

RESULT TABLE:

```
ENAME            SAL    0.75 * (SAL + 550)
--------     -------    ------------------
BLAKE        2850.00               2550.00
JONES        2975.00               2643.75
```

Write your answer here:

______

______

______

______

______

______

Exercise 2.5

Let's test the second ORDER BY rule mentioned in the previous exercise. Change Exercise 2.4 to order the results by the DEPTNO column.

RESULT TABLE:

```
ENAME          SAL    0.75 * (SAL + 550)
--------   -------    ------------------
JONES      2975.00               2643.75
BLAKE      2850.00               2550.00     phantom column    DEPTNO
```

Write your answer here:

Congratulations! You have just completed the workshop exercises for this chapter. If you would like to practice more commands in a simulated SQL environment, turn on your computer and choose Menu Item 1 from Exercise Disk 1. Good luck!

Solutions to Workshop Exercises

Exercise 2.1 - Solution

```
SELECT ENAME, SAL, SAL + 100, SAL - 100,
SAL * 1.267,  SAL / -1.267
FROM EMP  WHERE JOB = 'MANAGER';
```

Notes

This is basic SQL. Numeric expressions can use one of the four arithmetic operators:

- + for addition
- - for subtraction
- * for multiplication
- / for division

Each expression is separated from the others by a comma and produces one results column.

Also remember that - and + can be prefixes to a number or expression. For example, -(SAL-100) computes the difference between SAL and 100, and then reverses the sign of that difference. For a SAL of 400, -(400-100) is -300; but for a SAL of 50, -(50-100) is +50. A prefix of " + " does nothing to change the sign of the expression.

Exercise 2.2 - Solution

```
SELECT ENAME, SAL, 0.75 * (SAL + 550)
FROM EMP  WHERE JOB = 'MANAGER';
```

Notes

This example shows that the expression:

0.75 * (SAL + 550)

needs to use parentheses, forcing SQL to change the normal precedence order when calculating the result. The normal execution order is left to right, with multiplication or division done first and any addition or subtraction performed afterward. Without the parentheses, the expression above would be:

0.75 * SAL + 550

This is equivalent to:

(0.75 * SAL) + 550

This expression shows that the multiplication is completed first, then the 550 is added—not what we wanted. So be sure to use parentheses any time you mix " * / " with " + - ".

Exercise 2.3 - Solution

```
SELECT ENAME, SAL, 0.75 * (SAL + 550)
FROM EMP WHERE JOB = 'MANAGER'
AND (SAL + 550) * 0.75 > 2500;
```

Notes

You probably knew that the expression that we used in our SELECT clause could also be used to choose rows by including it in the WHERE clause. This simple inequality

(SAL + 550) * 0.75 > 2500

can be reduced to a simpler

(SAL + 550) > 3333.33

and to the basic logical predicate

SAL > 2783.33

This simpler form may actually process more quickly for a large table, but it is far removed from the business problem that was stated as "only for those with a new salary greater than 2500."

A more interesting predicate expression might involve two or more columns, as in:

((SAL * 0.75) - (COMM * 1.2)) > 1300.

As you can see, this is not as easily simplified, although it is the same as

(SAL * 0.75) > 1300 + (COMM * 1.2)

or even

SAL > 1733.33 + (COMM * 1.6)

Once again we've lost our "original meaning."

Exercise 2.4 - Solution

```
SELECT ENAME, SAL, 0.75 * (SAL + 550)
FROM EMP  WHERE JOB = 'MANAGER'
AND (SAL + 550) * 0.75 > 2500
ORDER BY 0.75 * (SAL + 550);
```

Notes

The use of an expression in an ORDER BY clause is not found or permitted in most SQL systems, but it is permissible in ORACLE. Other systems require that the ORDER BY clause contain only column names from the SELECT clause or position numbers. Position numbers are substituted for either column names or expressions of results columns from the SELECT clause. Our example is equivalent to

```
SELECT clause positions:
          1      2               3
        __|__   _|_   ___________|___________
SELECT ENAME, SAL, 0.75 * (SAL + 550)
FROM EMP
WHERE JOB = 'MANAGER'
AND (SAL + 550) * 0.75 > 2500
ORDER BY 3;                <——        3rd position
```

ORACLE extends the ORDER BY rules in two ways:

1. The ORDER BY clause can include an expression, not just a column name or position number.
2. The ORDER BY clause can include an expression or a column name that is not found in the SELECT clause.

Rule 1 above does not hold for UNION or for the other ORACLE relational operators, MINUS, and INTERSECT. For those three cases, use the position number syntax.

Exercise 2.5 - Solution

```
SELECT ENAME, SAL, 0.75 * (SAL + 550)
FROM EMP  WHERE JOB = 'MANAGER'
AND (SAL + 550) * 0.75 > 2500
ORDER BY DEPTNO;
```

Notes

The DEPTNO column is not found in the SELECT clause. Again, remember that this ORACLE feature is neither found nor permitted in the IBM SQL systems, nor in most others. Standard SQL requires that the columns named in the ORDER BY clause must also be specified in the SELECT clause for the query. (If you have access to any other SQL systems you could try this yourself.)

In order for ORACLE to perform this feat, the system must include the DEPTNO column in the data it fetches from the database, but not pass it on to the results table after the sorting operation is performed.

Once again, you can't use this feature with UNION, MINUS, or INTERSECT.

3

Advanced Use of Aggregate Functions

This chapter begins with a review of how groups are formed and how groups are used in aggregate functions. Next, the chapter discusses summary tables, the percentage of total calculation, and index usage. Finally, it covers outer join techniques that offer solutions to problems that occur when attempting to join tables.

REVIEWING GROUP BY AND HAVING

Let's review aggregate functions and how groups are formed and used. A group is a set of rows with one or more values in common.

The main use of groups in SQL is to allow one or more aggregate functions to be calculated for each group formed. Aggregate functions are also known as group functions and column functions.

Let's look at an example of the use of the GROUP BY clause.

```
                    GROUP BY DEPTNO, JOB

DEPTNO    JOB          SAL
------    --------     ----
    30    CLERK         950          — first group formed

    30    MANAGER      2850          — second group formed

    30    SALESMAN     1600          — third group formed
    30    SALESMAN     1250
    30    SALESMAN     1250
    30    SALESMAN     1500
```

First, the system uses the WHERE clause, such as WHERE DEPTNO IN 30, to filter out specific rows. The system takes those rows and sorts them by the values of the columns named in the GROUP BY list. This action forms groups. A group is produced for each set of rows having identical values.

Your results table will have one row for each group formed. Each results row is an aggregation of the rows that formed its group.

```
DEPTNO  JOB        SUM(SAL)   COUNT(*)
------  --------   --------   --------
    30  CLERK           950          1    —results for group 1
    30  MANAGER        2850          1    —results for group 2
    30  SALESMEN       5600          4    —results for group 3
```

You specify the GROUP BY syntax as follows:

```
SELECT <column_name(s)>, aggregate_function(s) (column_name(s))
FROM <table_name>
[WHERE <condition>]
GROUP BY <column_name(s)>
[HAVING <condition>]
[ORDER BY <column_name(s) / column_number(s)> [<ASC/DESC>]];
```

The SELECT clause may contain only three kinds of expressions when you use a GROUP BY:

1. Columns named in the GROUP BY list of columns
2. Aggregate functions (SUM, AVG, MIN, MAX, and COUNT) involving other columns in the tables
3. Constant expressions, such as 'IS THE AVERAGE' or 1985.

Example

You can see these three types of expressions in this typical query with GROUP BY:

```
SELECT JOB, AVG(SAL), '= Avg sal',
            COUNT(*), '= # of emp in job'
FROM EMP
WHERE JOB != 'PRESIDENT'
GROUP BY JOB;
```

The SELECT clause has:

A. Columns named in the GROUP BY list of columns.
B. Aggregate functions involving other columns in the table.
C. Constant expressions.

The results of this query are:

```
JOB        AVG(SAL)   '= Avg sal'  COUNT(*)  '= # of emp in job'
--------   ---------  -----------  --------  -------------------
ANALYST      3000.00  = Avg sal           2  = # of emp in job
CLERK        1037.50  = Avg sal           4  = # of emp in job
MANAGER      2758.33  = Avg sal           3  = # of emp in job
SALESMAN     1400.00  = Avg sal           4  = # of emp in job
```

A useful companion feature of GROUP BY is the HAVING clause. Just as the WHERE clause chooses only certain rows, HAVING chooses only certain groups to appear in the results.

The HAVING clause typically has a predicate (logical condition) that applies to the GROUP. The predicate may contain an aggregate function that is applied only to the rows in each group.

You cannot use an aggregate function in a WHERE clause. The WHERE clause predicate must apply to a single row.

Note: If you use the WHERE clause to filter rows out of the result before they are grouped and functions are performed on the groups, the system will process the query faster.

Let's modify the previous query to show only groups having an average salary less than $2500:

```
SELECT JOB, AVG(SAL), '= Avg sal',
            COUNT(*), '= # of emp in job'
FROM EMP
WHERE JOB != 'PRESIDENT'
GROUP BY JOB
HAVING AVG(SAL) < 2500;
```

As each group is formed, the AVG(SAL) is calculated for that group. If the predicate is TRUE (the logical condition is met), then the group is included in the results.

SUMMARY TABLES

Certain common calculations need to be done in two steps in SQL. Let's look at how summary tables can help.

A summary table is created to hold a set of values that are loaded from some other table in the database. You can use an INSERT statement with a sub-SELECT (an embedded SELECT statement) that contains an aggregate function and, perhaps, a GROUP BY clause. This inserts values, chosen by the sub-SELECT, into the summary table.

For example:

EMP_SAL

TOT_SALARY
29025

```
INSERT INTO EMP_SAL (TOT_SALARY)
   SELECT SUM(SAL)
   FROM EMP;
```

In the summary table EMP_SAL, there is a single column named TOT_SALARY. It has a single row. The row was inserted by the INSERT statement, which computed the SUM(SAL) value and placed it into the TOT_SALARY column.

One of the uses of summary tables is to reduce the amount of GROUP BY processing for frequently asked questions like "What is our total payroll?".

The INSERT statement used to load values is not commonly used:

```
Target table ─────┐
                  │
     INSERT INTO EMP_SAL (TOT_SALARY)       — list of columns
          SELECT          SUM(SAL)          — SELECT clause
          FROM EMP;                           expressions
                  │
Source table ─────┘
```

This format of the INSERT statement starts with the name of the target table (the table to receive the rows). This is followed by a list of columns in the target table. Any column not listed must support NULL values and is assigned a NULL value.

The remainder of the statement is a sub-SELECT that chooses data from one or more source tables. The SELECT clause must contain one expression (of a matching data type) for each target table column. The sub-SELECT may have WHERE, GROUP BY, or HAVING clauses, but not UNION or ORDER BY.

PERCENTAGE OF TOTAL

Here is a common calculation that takes two steps in SQL. The salary value contained in a row sometimes needs to be shown as a percentage of the total in the department or of the whole table:

```
     SAL    PCT_OF_TOTAL
--------    ------------
    1000            10.0
    2000            20.0
    3000            30.0
    4000            40.0
========    ============
   10000           100.0
```

```
Note: Hypothetical data
have been used for these
examples.
```

Currently, this type of calculation cannot be accomplished in one step in SQL. (It may be provided in front-end processors such as SQL*Plus, FOCUS, Query Management Facility, NOMAD, etc.)

To obtain percentage of total, use a summary table that contains the total value.

You join the detail data with the summary data from the summary table:

```
          from EMP                            from EMP_SAL
             |                                      |
  -----------+--------- results --------------------+---
  |        SAL                |           TOT_SALARY    |
  -------------------------------------------------------
          1000                               10000
          2000                               10000
          3000                               10000
          4000                               10000
```

```
SELECT E.SAL, S.TOT_SALARY
FROM EMP E, EMP_SAL S;                    — No join predicate
```

This forms a simple cartesian product with the one-row table by intentionally leaving off a join predicate. In this case a cartesian product is acceptable because of the small table size.

The calculation of a percentage of a salary in a group to the group's total salary can be done with a revised SELECT clause:

```
SELECT E.SAL, 100.0 * E.SAL / S.TOT_SALARY
FROM EMP E, EMP_SAL S;
```

SAL	EXPRESSION
1000	10.0
2000	20.0
3000	30.0
4000	40.0

Example

Suppose you want to know what percentage Smith's salary is of the total salaries of his department. To calculate the percentage, use a revised SELECT clause:

DEPT_AVG

DEPTNO	D_AVG_SAL
10	2916.66
20	2175.00
30	1566.66

```
INSERT INTO DEPT_AVG
  (DEPTNO, D_AVG_SAL)
SELECT DEPTNO, AVG(SAL)
FROM EMP
GROUP BY DEPTNO;
```

In this case, one row is inserted into the summary table DEPT_AVG for each group formed by DEPTNO.

A variation of the summary table would include a date column. Such a summary table would record sales or expenses within given time periods, such as weeks or months.

Look at the summary table below. It was designed to summarize quarterly sales by product.

PROD_SALES

PRODNO	QUARTER	SALES_TOT$
1001	198401	4622

Load new rows from a SALES table each quarter with:

```
INSERT INTO PROD_SALES
      (PRODNO, QUARTER, SALES_TOT$)
SELECT PRODNO, 198401, SUM(SALES$)
FROM SALES
WHERE SALE_DATE BETWEEN '01-JAN-1984' AND
      '31-MAR-1984'
GROUP BY PRODNO;
```

Include a constant in the INSERT statement and an appropriate WHERE clause in the sub-SELECT to retrieve values within the appropriate range of dates.

INDEX USAGE

An index is a compact file containing information called pointers about the physical location of records in a database.

Many of the features you have learned about (such as joins, subqueries, and GROUP BY) are performed by the RDBMS, even if there is no index available to speed up access to the tables. RDBMSs read every row in a table in the absence of an index.

If there is an index, then the system may choose to use it. Different systems may or may not use an available index for a particular type of predicate, such as IN or BETWEEN.

The review that follows should be helpful.

An index may speed up a query if it is a SELECT. If there is more than one INDEX for a table, the system chooses only the best one to use for most SELECTs.

You should be aware that when you do maintenance operations—INSERT, UPDATE, and DELETE—the indexes have to be maintained also, which slows down the system.

Having more indexes in a table is not always better.

To create an index on a table (you may need to have the INDEX privilege), issue the CREATE INDEX statement:

```
CREATE [UNIQUE] INDEX <index_name>
ON <table_name> (<column_name(s)> [ASC / DESC];
```

A UNIQUE INDEX ensures that the system won't allow more than one row to have any one key value.

An index can be used to locate just the row or set of rows needed for a query. Another use of an index is to speed up certain aggregate functions.

If you have an index on SAL, SUM(SAL) for the entire table can be calculated quickly by adding up the index entries. You could perform COUNT(*) for all rows using any index.

MIN(SAL) or MAX(SAL) for the whole table is quickly calculated using the index on SAL.

Define a multicolumn index:

```
CREATE INDEX EMPX1 ON EMP
(JOB ASC, EMPNO ASC, ENAME ASC)
```

The system gets results from the index if you do a query with a SELECT clause

```
SELECT ENAME, EMPNO, JOB FROM EMP ...
```

This is usually faster than getting the results from the data rows.

OUTER JOIN TECHNIQUES

The join operation is a powerful feature of SQL. Remember to name two or more tables in the FROM clause. Include a join predicate to link rows having equal values in a certain column or columns. (By the way, joins may be performed using inequalities, but these joins are not common.)

A problem occurs when you attempt to join two tables, one of which does not have a matching row for some row in the other table. This is known as the outer join problem.

Here is an example. Suppose we need to produce a report showing how many employees are in each department:

```
DEPTNO    DNAME               COUNT(*)
------    ----------------    --------
    10    ACCOUNTING                 3
  etc.
```

Think for a moment how you would use SQL features to produce this report.

You need to join the DEPT table, which has the DNAME column, with the EMP table. Then, you need to GROUP BY department to produce a count of rows in each department.

The SQL query is:

```
SELECT D.DEPTNO, D.DNAME, COUNT(*)
FROM DEPT D, EMP E
WHERE D.DEPTNO = E.DEPTNO
GROUP BY D.DEPTNO, D.DNAME;
```

You might be surprised to find that the GROUP BY clause has two columns. To include both D.DEPTNO and D.DNAME in the SELECT clause, you need to GROUP BY both columns. Notice that both columns change values together.

```
SELECT D.DEPTNO, D.DNAME, COUNT(*)
FROM DEPT D, EMP E
WHERE D.DEPTNO = E.DEPTNO    —— join predicate
GROUP BY D.DEPTNO, D.DNAME;
```

The system relies on the join predicate to combine a DEPT row with each EMP row having the same DEPTNO value.

Your sample table has one row for Department 40:

```
DEPTNO  DNAME          LOC
------  -----------    ----------
    40    OPERATION      BOSTON
```

What happens when we try to join this row with our EMP rows? There are no employees yet for Department 40. The join won't produce any row in our answer.

Here is an answer that includes the row:

```
DEPTNO  DNAME                  COUNT(*)
------  ----------------       --------
    40  OPERATIONS                    0
```

The solution to this outer join problem is not straightforward, unless you use an RDBMS that has a special syntax to handle it.

ORACLE has the following technique:

```
SELECT D.DEPTNO, D.DNAME, COUNT(*)
FROM DEPT D, EMP E
WHERE D.DEPTNO = E.DEPTNO (+)    ← ORACLE syntax
GROUP BY D.DEPTNO, D.DNAME;
```

The symbol (+) tells the ORACLE system to append NULL values to a row in the D table, if the E table has no matching values.

There is another technique for handling the outer join problem. It involves using the UNION operation in SQL.

UNION allows you to combine two or more SELECT statements and their results. Rows from each SELECT statement are "stacked" after each other. Then the rows are sorted to eliminate duplicate results.

UNION ALL is an alternate form of UNION that skips the sort and leaves duplicates.

The SELECT clauses must conform to the same number of expressions and they must have matching data types.

The following example shows this.

```
SELECT A, B, 1 FROM TABLE1 WHERE ...
UNION
SELECT X, Y, 2 FROM TABLE2 WHERE ....
ORDER BY 3, 1;
```

Both queries have three expressions in the SELECT clause.

Here X must have the same general data type as A. Also, Y must match data types with B. Most systems allow some leeway in data type matching. For example, both data types must be some numeric type or both must be some character string type.

The optional ORDER BY clause must use the integer format to identify expressions.

The following SQL technique deals with the outer join problem. Here use UNION to add a second SELECT statement. The results of the two queries are combined into one table.

```
SELECT D.DEPTNO, D.DNAME, COUNT(*)
FROM DEPT D, EMP E
WHERE D.DEPTNO = E.DEPTNO
GROUP BY D.DEPTNO, D.DNAME

UNION

 SELECT DEPTNO, DNAME, 0
 FROM DEPT
 WHERE DEPTNO NOT IN
   (SELECT DISTINCT DEPTNO FROM EMP);
```

If a subquery finds no matching values for DEPTNO, each row is assigned the value zero in the COUNT(*) column.

In this chapter, you learned how to:

- Use summary tables in calculations requiring two steps
- Identify the percentage of total calculation
- Issue the CREATE INDEX command
- Explain the techniques that deal with the outer join problem

Here are some Workshop Exercises to hone your new skills.

Workshop Exercises

Advanced Use of Aggregate Functions

You're ready to practice using aggregate functions. In this section, you will practice the following concepts:

1. The use of aggregate functions
2. The use of the GROUP BY and HAVING clauses
3. The use of summary tables
4. Percentage of total
5. The use of CREATE INDEX
6. The use of outer joins

Exercise 3.1

A useful technique is to run an SQL query against an unfamiliar table to obtain counts of various categories. Show all the job titles and the breakdown of how many employees are in each title by department.

RESULT TABLE:

```
JOB          DEPTNO    COUNT(*)
---------    ------    --------
ANALYST          20           2
CLERK            10           1
CLERK            20           2
CLERK            30           1
MANAGER          10           1
MANAGER          20           1
MANAGER          30           1
PRESIDENT        10           1
SALESMAN         30           4
```

Write your answer here:

____

____

____

____

____

____

Exercise 3.2

Show which jobs in which department have a staffing of two or more employees. (Hint: Add a new clause to the answer in Exercise 3.1.)

RESULT TABLE:

```
JOB          DEPTNO    COUNT(*)
---------    ------    --------
ANALYST          20           2
CLERK            20           2
SALESMAN         30           4
```

Write your answer here:

____

____

____

____

____

____

Exercise 3.3

Show which jobs in which department have a staffing of two or more employees, but show the highest staff levels first. If more than one has the same level, list in department sequence too. (Hint: Add another clause to the answer in Exercise 3.2.)

RESULT TABLE:

```
JOB          DEPTNO    COUNT(*)
--------     ------    --------
ANALYST          20           2
CLERK            20           2
SALESMAN         30           4
```

Write your answer here:

____

____

____

____

____

____

Exercise 3.4

In this exercise, we will use a table called TEMP1.

Show the percentage of each employee's SAL to the total of the firm's salaries. Use EMPNO, ENAME, SAL, "PCT" as the columns. (Hint: Step 1 is to load a row into TEMP1 (with NUMB = 0) with the total of all SAL values. Step 2 is to solve the problem with a join.)

RESULT TABLE:

```
1 record created.

EMPNO     ENAME      SAL      PCT
-----     ------     ----     -------
7369      SMITH       800     2.75624
7499      ALLEN      1600     5.51249
7521      WARD       1250     4.30663
7566      JONES      2975     10.2498
7654      MARTIN     1250     4.30663
7698      BLAKE      2850     9.81912
7782      CLARK      2450       8.441
7788      SCOTT      3000     10.3359
7839      KING       5000     17.2265
7844      TURNER     1500     5.16796
7876      ADAMS      1100     3.78984
7900      JAMES       950     3.27304
7902      FORD       3000     10.3359
7934      MILLER     1300      4.4789
```

Write your answer here:

Exercise 3.5

For this exercise we would need to do some housekeeping again, to empty table TEMP1.

We would enter DELETE FROM TEMP1. SELECT * FROM TEMP1 would yield an empty table.

Now, show for each department, the DEPTNO, DNAME, and total departmental salaries over 2000 with "TOT HI SAL" as the column name. After you produce this report, load the DEPTNO and SUM data into the TEMP1 table columns. (Hint: Use INSERT to load rows into TEMP1 with NUMB receiving DEPTNO.)

RESULT TABLE:

```
DEPTNO   DNAME          TOT HI SAL
------   ----------     ----------
    10   ACCOUNTING           7450
    20   RESEARCH             8975
    30   SALES                2850
```

Write your answer here:

___

___

___

___

___

___

Exercise 3.6

Let's repeat Exercise 3.5 using table TEMP1 instead of the GROUP BY clause. Recall that TEMP1 has the following values in its columns.

```
column name:     NUMB      CALC
                 ------    -------------------------
value:           DEPTNO    SUM(SAL) where SAL > 2000
```

Show for each department the DEPTNO, DNAME, and total departmental salaries over 2000 with "TOT HI SAL" as the column name.

RESULT TABLE:

DEPTNO	DNAMETOT	HI SAL
10	ACCOUNTING	7450
20	RESEARCH	8975
30	SALES	2850

Write your answer here:

______

______

______

______

______

______

Exercise 3.7

Here is the final progression in this series of exercises. Show for each department the DEPTNO, DNAME, and total salary as "TOT SAL." Alongside, show the total of departmental salaries over 2000 as "HI SAL" and the percentage of those high salaries to the department's total salary as "HI PCT." (Hint: Use TEMP1 for the HI SAL values.)

RESULT TABLE:

DEPTNO	DNAME	TOT SAL	HI SAL	HI PCT
10	ACCOUNTING	8750	7450	85.1429
20	RESEARCH	10875	8975	82.5287
30	SALES	9400	2850	30.3191

Write your answer here:

____

____

____

____

____

____

Exercise 3.8

To speed up processing on a large table, or to ensure unique values for the key column or columns, we can provide an index. Create an index "TEMP1X" on the NUMB column of TEMP1. Make it unique. (Hint: CREATE ... INDEX ON ... (...);.)

RESULT:

```
Index created.
```

Write your answer here:

____

____

____

____

____

____

Exercise 3.9

Try this outer join exercise. Show all departments and the employee with the JOB 'MANAGER' assigned to that department. List DEPTNO, DNAME, EMPNO, ENAME, JOB. (Hint: Use the ORACLE outer join feature " =...(+) ".)

RESULT TABLE:

```
DEPTNO  DNAME        EMPNO  ENAME   JOB
------  ----------   -----  -----   --------------
    10  ACCOUNTING    7782  CLARK   MANAGER
    20  RESEARCH      7566  JONES   MANAGER
    30  SALES         7698  BLAKE   MANAGER
    40  OPERATIONS
```

Write your answer here:

You've completed this chapter on the use of aggregate functions. To try some exercises in a simulated SQL environment, choose Menu Item 2 from Exercise Disk 1.

Solutions to Workshop Exercises

Exercise 3.1 - Solution

```
SELECT JOB, DEPTNO, COUNT(*)
FROM EMP
GROUP BY JOB, DEPTNO;
```

Notes

The main purpose of the GROUP BY function is to perform aggregation operations. (Aggregation operations are column functions like SUM, AVG, MIN, MAX, and COUNT.) When you use GROUP BY, the aggregations are done after groups are formed.

To form groups of rows having JOB and DEPTNO with the same values, the SQL system uses an internal sorting process (similar to ORDER BY JOB, DEPTNO). The sort places the rows into groups with the identical JOB and DEPTNO values. Then the column function COUNT(*) is computed for each group.

We can form groups from among all the rows in a table (or a join of tables), or we can first request a subset of rows with the WHERE clause.

Here's a quick restatement of the rules when coding an SQL statement with GROUP BY. The SELECT clause can have some or all of these items:

- Columns named in the GROUP BY list of columns
- Column functions involving other columns in the table
- Constant expressions

In our answer, groups are formed for each pairing of JOB and DEPTNO. This allows us to answer the request but only for the groups actually formed.

If a certain job (e.g., ANALYST) doesn't appear in Department 10, for example, there won't be the entry "ANALYST, 10: 0", which you might have wanted. That result would be the product of a true "cross-tabulation" tool, which SQL cannot exactly match.

Exercise 3.2 - Solution

```
SELECT JOB, DEPTNO, COUNT(*)
FROM EMP
GROUP BY JOB, DEPTNO
HAVING COUNT(*) > 1;
```

Notes

Without the last clause (the HAVING clause), our query presents results with all groups. We need to limit the groups that are included in the results. The HAVING clause is used to choose groups after they are formed (in much the same way as the WHERE clause chooses rows).

```
HAVING COUNT(*) > 1
```

HAVING may use a column function (but WHERE may not). Here we have applied the column function COUNT(*), meaning "the number of rows," to each group formed. Only groups with more than one participant are retained for the results.

We might have used the alternate specification,

```
HAVING COUNT(*) >= 2
```

which accomplishes the same result.

Exercise 3.3 - Solution

```
SELECT JOB, DEPTNO, COUNT(*)
FROM EMP
GROUP BY JOB, DEPTNO
HAVING COUNT(*) > 1
ORDER BY 3,2;
```

Notes

The GROUP BY does a sort or may use an index to avoid an extra sorting step. You can guarantee that the GROUP BY sequence will be used by adding an ORDER BY with those same columns specified. For instance, if you had:

```
GROUP BY JOB, DEPTNO
```

you would specify ORDER BY JOB, DEPTNO to ensure the same ordering (no matter how the system works in the future).

If you want your results in a sequence other than that returned by GROUP BY, then you should add an ORDER BY clause as shown in the solution above.

Most SQL systems don't allow "ORDER BY COUNT(*)", so we used the alternate format, "ORDER BY 3," where " 3 " is the position of the expression in the SELECT clause.

Exercise 3.4 - Solution

Step 1:

```
INSERT INTO TEMP1 (NUMB, CALC)
SELECT 0, SUM(SAL) FROM EMP;
```

Step 2:

```
SELECT E.EMPNO, E.ENAME, E.SAL, 100 *
E.SAL / T.CALC "PCT"
FROM EMP E, TEMP1 T;
```

Notes

Certain calculations need to be done in two steps because SQL does not hold temporary values.

In Step 1 above, we use the "Format 2" of the INSERT statement to load our temporary table. (Format 1 INSERT supplies a list of individual VALUES for a single row.) The Format 2 INSERT uses a SELECT statement against one or more source tables. It loads the results of the SELECT into rows of the target table.

The expressions "0," a constant, and "SUM(SAL)," are in the SELECT clause. They are loaded into the NUMB and CALC columns respectively:

```
INSERT INTO TEMP1        (NUMB,     CALC)   <—— target table
                            |          |
source table ——>    SELECT 0,   SUM(SAL) FROM EMP
```

We insert the zero to fill up the NUMB column, which has no function in this example.

Step 2 is a special form of a cartesian product. We know there is only one row in the source table TEMP1. This join without a join predicate appends the single row of TEMP1 next to each row of the EMP table.

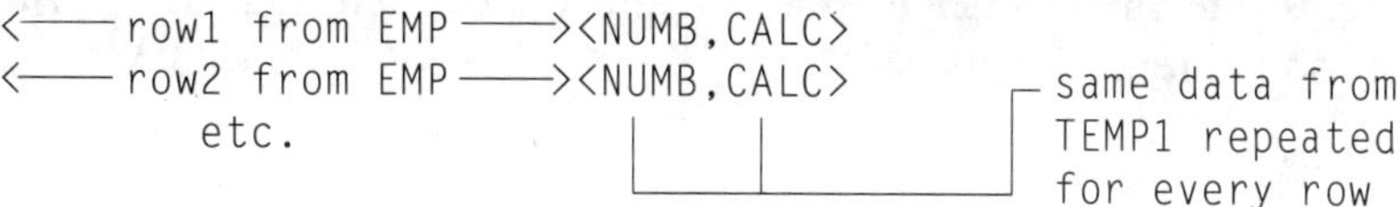

Exercise 3.5 - Solution

Step 1:

```
SELECT D.DEPTNO, D.DNAME,
SUM(E.SAL) "TOT HI SAL"
FROM DEPT D, EMP E
WHERE D.DEPTNO = E.DEPTNO
AND E.SAL > 2000
GROUP BY D.DEPTNO, D.DNAME;
```

Step 2:

```
INSERT INTO TEMP1 (NUMB, CALC)
SELECT DEPTNO, SUM(SAL) FROM EMP
WHERE SAL > 2000
GROUP BY DEPTNO;
```

Notes

This exercise lays the groundwork for the next exercise. But first there are a few things worth reviewing in these two answers.

The SELECT statement for Step 1 has a GROUP BY. The grouping is on two columns because we need the two columns presented in the SELECT clause.

Notice that in Step 2 there is also grouping, but only with one column. This time we're using the NUMB column in TEMP1 to hold "DEPTNO" values. The subselect is grouping by DEPTNO because we want to load DEPTNO and the SUM(SAL) for each department into the two columns of TEMP1.

What would have happened if we had made the GROUP BY in Step 2 be the same DEPTNO, DNAME as in Step 1? In this case, that would have worked identically to our solution because whenever DEPTNO changes, DNAME changes along with it.

Please notice that the summary table concept can use data from most any SELECT statement (except ones containing UNION). This includes joins, grouping, and those subqueries that don't reference the table into which you are inserting.

If you need such a self-referencing INSERT, you'll have to do it in two steps, the first INSERT to a temporary table and then to the final target table (also referenced in the subquery).

Exercise 3.6 - Solution

```
SELECT D.DEPTNO, D.DNAME,
T.CALC "TOT HI SAL"
FROM DEPT D, TEMP1 T
WHERE D.DEPTNO = T.NUMB
ORDER BY D.DEPTNO;
```

Notes

We have replaced a complex join that included grouping with a join. The grouping had already occurred when we loaded the summary table using the INSERT in Exercise 3.5, Step 2.

Most likely the join on DEPTNO would have resulted in the results' being sequenced by DEPTNO. The ORDER BY clause was added to ensure that the sequence was the same as GROUP BY DEPTNO, etc.

The join predicate was tricky: D.DEPTNO = T.NUMB, not T.DEPTNO. We had placed the DEPTNO values into the T.NUMB column so we would have a linkage from TEMP1 to the other tables by department number.

Exercise 3.7 - Solution

```
SELECT D.DEPTNO, D.DNAME, SUM(E.SAL) "TOT SAL",
T.CALC "HI SAL", 100 * T.CALC/SUM(E.SAL) "HI PCT"
FROM DEPT D, EMP E, TEMP1 T
WHERE D.DEPTNO = E.DEPTNO
AND D.DEPTNO = T.NUMB
GROUP BY D.DEPTNO, D.DNAME, T.CALC;
```

Notes

This answer demonstrates that you can't show aggregations by "apples and oranges" in the same query unless you use separate summary tables. In this example:

1. The main query is summing all rows by DEPTNO.
2. The summary table has only certain rows summed by DEPTNO.

If this answer had needed a "WHERE SAL > 2000" to satisfy number 2 above, it would have applied also to number 1 and resulted in a wrong answer.

Let's review the interesting parts of this problem together. Remember that in TEMP1 we had:

```
column name:     NUMB      CALC
                 ------    ---------------------------
value:           DEPTNO    SUM(SAL) where SAL > 2000
```

We joined DEPT, EMP, and TEMP1 by the DEPTNO value:

```
<——— DEPT ———><——— EMP ———><——— TEMP———>
 (DEPTNO)  (DNAME)     (SAL)  (DEPTNO)    (NUMB) (CALC)
   |                             |          |      |
   |____________ = ______________|          |__ = _|
```

For example, for Department 20, the join produces these five rows:

```
        DEPT                    EMP                  TEMP1
-------------------       ---------------        -----------
DEPTNO     DNAME          SAL     DEPTNO         NUMB   CALC
------     --------       ----    ------         ----   ----
    20     RESEARCH        800        20           20   8975
    20     RESEARCH       3000        20           20   8975
    20     RESEARCH       2975        20           20   8975
    20     RESEARCH       1100        20           20   8975
    20     RESEARCH       3000        20           20   8975
```

If we ignore the duplicate DEPTNO values, including NUMB, there are three columns in the join that are constant values for each DEPTNO: DEPTNO, DNAME, and CALC. The other column is SAL, which changes for each of the five employees.

We use this GROUP BY clause,

```
GROUP BY D.DEPTNO, D.NAME, T.CALC
```

which includes the three constant-value columns for each DEPTNO.

We've noted before that multiple related columns can go in the GROUP BY clause if they change together and if they are needed in the SELECT clause.

What's left is to SUM the SAL column for each DEPTNO group:

```
SELECT D.DEPTNO, D.DNAME,
SUM(E.SAL), T.CALC,
100 * T.CALC / SUM(E.SAL) "HI PCT"
```

The last expression above, "HI PCT," is the "percentage of those high salaries to the department's total salary." We could do the calculation because the sum of high salaries had been reduced to a constant by the INSERT process done earlier in Exercise 3.5, Step 2.

A final question: How could we have shown the count of high-salaried employees in this query along with their aggregate salaries?

If our TEMP1 table had included another column (e.g., CALC2), we could have loaded that column with COUNT(*) at the same time we loaded CALC with SUM(SAL). Our grouping above would have been:

```
GROUP BY D.DEPTNO, D.NAME, T.CALC, T.CALC2
```

because the T.CALC2 value would also be a constant for each DEPTNO.

If many applications request the same aggregate numbers throughout the day (for instance, last month's sales by product), it may pay to create summary tables derived from the detail tables. The summary tables could be reloaded each night (or as needed) and save processing time for each subsequent query needing the data. This summary table technique might even suffice for "real-time" data, which could be summarized hourly.

Exercise 3.8 - Solution

```
CREATE UNIQUE INDEX TEMP1X ON TEMP1
(NUMB);
```

Notes

The index is created on one or more key columns. In this case the single key column is "NUMB." A UNIQUE INDEX ensures that the system won't allow more than one row to have any one value of NUMB, the key of the index.

Once an index is created, leave it up to the SQL system to use the index, to use some other index, or to use no index to perform SQL operations most efficiently. Unlike other data management systems, we do not specify an index name for a query.

If we left out the "UNIQUE" option:

```
CREATE INDEX TEMP1X ON TEMP1 (NUMB);
```

the system would allow rows to be inserted even when more than one row has the same key value.

Exercise 3.9 - Solution

```
SELECT D.DEPTNO, D.DNAME,
E.EMPNO, E.ENAME, E.JOB
FROM DEPT D, EMP E
WHERE D.DEPTNO = E.DEPTNO (+)
AND (E.JOB = 'MANAGER' OR E.JOB IS NULL);
```

Notes

Here's a quick review of the outer join problem with SQL, and how ORACLE provides a solution.

A problem occurs whenever you attempt to join two tables if one of the tables does not have a matching row for a row in the other table.

The system relies on the join predicate:

```
WHERE D.DEPTNO = E.DEPTNO
```

to actually combine a DEPT row with each EMP row having the same DEPTNO value. Your ORACLE sample DEPT table has one row for Department 40, but there are no EMP table employees yet for Department 40. The join won't produce any row in the answer.

ORACLE provides the following technique:

```
SELECT ....
FROM DEPT D, EMP E
WHERE D.DEPTNO = E.DEPTNO (+)
....
```

If the EMP table has no matching values, the symbol (+) tells the ORACLE system to append an EMP table row with all NULL values to the unmatched row in the DEPT table. With this outer join, the results contains the row:

```
DEPTNO  DNAME        EMPNO  ENAME  JOB
------  ----------   -----  -----  ---------
    40  OPERATIONS
```

On the results line shown above, the JOB has a NULL value, so we added to our query the predicate:

```
... OR E.JOB IS NULL
```

In other queries, you could even test for missing rows (without using NOT IN or NOT EXISTS) by using the fact that the unmatched row will have a NULL column:

```
SELECT ....
FROM DEPT D, EMP E
WHERE D.DEPTNO = E.DEPTNO (+)
AND E.EMPNO IS NULL
```

4

Advanced Subqueries

In this chapter you will learn about the use of subqueries in complex queries. This lesson also covers SQL features such as ANY, ALL, EXISTS, and NOT EXISTS.

COMPLEX QUERIES

Here is a review of complex queries, specifically those with multiple predicates in the WHERE clause.

Standard SQL uses the following predicate types in the WHERE clause:

- Logical comparisons
- IN (list of values)
- BETWEEN (range of values)
- LIKE search string
- NULL value test

Let's review each type.

Logical predicates (conditions in a WHERE clause) contain two expressions to be compared using any of the logical comparison operators:

equal (=) or not equal to (!=, ^=, <>)
greater than (>) or greater than or equal to (>=, !<, ^<)
less than (<) or less than or equal to (<=, !>, ^>)

Here are three examples of logical predicates:

```
SAL >= 2500
```

This logical predicate finds rows containing SAL values that are greater than or equal to 2500.

```
SAL <> COMM
```

This one finds rows containing SAL values and COMM values that are not equal to each other.

```
DEPT = (subquery returning a DEPTNO value)
```

And this finds rows matching a single value of DEPTNO returned by a subquery.

If you want to choose rows with DEPTNO values of 30 or 40, the predicates would need to be complete. The predicate:

```
DEPTNO = 30 or 40
```

is incomplete. The complete and correct predicate is:

```
DEPTNO = 30 OR DEPTNO = 40
```

The set comparison operator IN is shorthand for "equal to any of these values."

Here is an example of how to use IN when the data type is numeric:

```
DEPTNO IN (30, 40)
```

This predicate is the equivalent of:

```
DEPTNO IN 30 OR DEPTNO IN 40
```

Here is an example of how to use IN with character values:

```
ENAME IN ('Faith', 'Hope', 'Charity')
```

This predicate chooses rows having ENAME values equal to any of the three values specified in the list.

When you want to find row values within a designated range of values, use two logical predicates connected by AND:

```
SAL >= 2000 AND SAL <= 2500
```

The BETWEEN predicate is a shortcut:

```
SAL BETWEEN 2000 AND 2500
```

This will choose rows with SAL values from 2000 to 2500 inclusive.

The LIKE predicate allows partial comparisons, such as "starting with (a character string)," "ending with (a character string)," or "containing (a character string)." The LIKE predicate operates only on columns containing character values.

You can use two special characters in your search string. The search string must be enclosed in apostrophes.

When using the LIKE predicate to search for specific values in a particular range, you can employ a "wildcard" to designate the range. The underscore symbol "_" is your wildcard. Use one underscore to designate one undetermined character.

For example, the predicate **'LIKE AB__'** chooses rows containing values four characters long, starting with **AB**, with the first character A and the second character B. The third and fourth characters can be any character. An acceptable value returned for the column ENAME is "ABLE".

LIKE uses another special character as a wildcard. The % (percent) represents zero or more characters.

The predicate **LIKE 'M%cDonald'** chooses rows containing the character values "McDonald" and "MacDonald".

The predicate **LIKE '%and%'** will choose rows containing character values with "and" anywhere in the value string. Rows containing the values "and," "sand," and "branding" would be retrieved.

Use NOT with each of the predicate types to get a negative value. Place NOT within the predicate or in front of it, as shown in this table:

Positive	Negative	Alternate Negative
A > B		NOT A > B
A IN (list of values)	A NOT IN (list of values)	NOT A IN (list of values)
A BETWEEN B AND C	A NOT BETWEEN B AND C	NOT A BETWEEN B AND C
A LIKE 'string'	A NOT LIKE 'string'	NOT A LIKE 'string'
A IS NULL	A IS NOT NULL	NOT A IS NULL

You can combine predicates with AND, OR, AND NOT or OR NOT operators. Expressions involving logical comparison operators, AND, OR, and NOT are evaluated in the following order. These are called the rules of precedence.

1. All of the logical comparison operators have EQUAL precedence:

```
=    !=    ^=    <>   >=   <    <=   BETWEEN...AND   IN   LIKE IS NULL
```

2. NOT
3. AND
4. OR

The order in which calculations or expressions are executed is referred to as the rules of precedence. Operations involving operators of equal precedence are evaluated from left to right.

To override the rules of precedence, enclose expressions in parentheses. Expressions in parentheses are always evaluated first.

Let's look at an example using several operators.

```
WHERE SAL > 2000 OR DEPTNO IN(30, 40)
AND NOT ENAME LIKE '%ER'
```

This is the equivalent of:

```
WHERE SAL > 2000
OR
(DEPTNO IN(30, 40)
AND
(NOT ENAME LIKE '%ER'))
```

This complex search condition chooses rows with either a SAL value of more than 2000, or both a DEPTNO value of 30 or 40 and a name not ending with ER.

Use parentheses to force the SQL system to do exactly what you want.

You can also place NOT before a parenthesized search condition. Here are two examples:

```
AND NOT (<predicate_1> OR <predicate_2>)
WHERE NOT (<predicate_1> AND <predicate_2>)
```

If a predicate matches a row value and a row is retrieved from the table in question, then the predicate is "true."

For example, if the SAL column for one row of BONUS contains a value of 800, the predicate:

```
WHERE SAL = 800
```

matches the row value, and the row is retrieved. The predicate is true.

If a predicate does not match a row value, the predicate is "false."

For our SAL value of 800, the predicate:

```
WHERE SAL BETWEEN 1500 AND 2000
```

does not match the row value (800 is not between 1500 and 2000). The predicate is false.

A predicate can also return an unknown result, in the case of NULL (unknown, undefined) values.

If a row in BONUS contains a NULL value in the COMM column, the predicate:

```
WHERE COMM > 1200
```

does not match the row value. It is not known if COMM is greater than 1200, because COMM itself is unknown. So the row is not retrieved, because the predicate is unknown.

If predicates are used in combinations of two or more, they follow this table:

Predicate A	Predicate B	A OR B	A AND B
TRUE	TRUE	TRUE	TRUE
TRUE	FALSE	TRUE	FALSE
TRUE	?U?	TRUE	?U?
FALSE	TRUE	TRUE	FALSE
FALSE	FALSE	FALSE	FALSE
FALSE	?U?	?U?	FALSE
?U?	TRUE	TRUE	?U?
?U?	FALSE	?U?	FALSE
?U?	?U?	?U?	?U?

Only true results are presented when the results of a query are displayed.

Notice that with the **OR** operator, if either predicate is true, the result is true.

With the **AND** operator, both predicates must be true for the result to be true.

An unknown predicate or a true predicate returns a true result. All other combinations of unknown predicates return a result of false or unknown, and no row is retrieved.

SUBQUERIES

Let's look at how to use subqueries in complex queries.

In combining predicates using NOT, AND, and OR, you produce complex queries. Any of the predicates combined with these operators may contain a subquery.

First, let's look at subqueries.

A **subquery** is a separate SELECT statement enclosed in parentheses. This SELECT statement may include any SQL feature except UNION and ORDER BY.

Here is a diagram of the placement of a typical subquery within a query:

```
SELECT ...                                Main
FROM ...                                  Query
WHERE <condition>  (Subquery)
```

The subquery is executed first, and a temporary result is held in memory. The temporary result supplies a value or set of values for the condition in the main query. This value, or values, is checked against the condition in the main query to determine if a row should be retrieved for display.

Let's look at two examples of subqueries.

Example

If your boss says, "Show me the employees who work out of Dallas," display that information using the following query and subquery:

```
SELECT*
FROM EMP
WHERE DEPTNO IN
               (SELECT DEPTNO FROM DEPT
                 WHERE LOC = 'DALLAS');
```

The subquery, enclosed in parentheses, returns a list of departments located in Dallas. This list is used by the predicate WHERE DEPTNO IN to determine if a row from EMP should be retrieved.

Example

Here is another example.

"Which employees earn less than the average salary?"

```
SELECT*
FROM EMP
WHERE SAL <
           (SELECT AVG(SAL)
            FROM EMP);
```

The subquery is executed first, returning a single value, the average of all salaries in the EMP table. The main query then selects rows from EMP that contain a salary value less than the average.

Subqueries may be used in more than one predicate. Here is a diagram of the placement of subqueries in more than one predicate:

```
SELECT *
FROM ...
WHERE <condition_1> (subquery_1)
AND   <condition_2> (subquery_2);
```

An example of the above format is:

```
SELECT *
FROM EMP
WHERE DEPTNO IN (SELECT DEPTNO FROM DEPT
                 WHERE LOC = 'DALLAS')
AND SAL = (SELECT MAX(SAL)
           FROM BONUS);
```

A subquery itself may contain one or more subqueries. Here is a diagram of the placement of subqueries within subqueries:

```
SELECT *
FROM ...
WHERE <condition_1> (subquery_1)
AND   <condition_2> (subquery_2);
```

Subquery_2 can itself contain a subquery:

```
(SELECT ...
 FROM ...
 WHERE  <condition_3> (subquery_3))
```

Here is an example in the previous format:

```
SELECT *
FROM EMP
WHERE DEPTNO IN (SELECT DEPTNO FROM DEPT
                 WHERE LOC = 'DALLAS')
AND JOB IN (SELECT JOB
            FROM BONUS
            WHERE ENAME IN (SELECT ENAME
                            FROM EMP
                            WHERE MGR = 7839));
```

Example

```
SELECT * FROM EMP
 WHERE SAL <
           (SELECT AVG(SAL)
            FROM EMP)
 AND DEPTNO IN
     (SELECT DEPTNO FROM DEPT
      WHERE LOC =
                 (SELECT LOC FROM DEPT
                  WHERE DEPTNO =
                               (SELECT DEPTNO FROM EMP
                                WHERE ENAME = 'BLAKE')));
```

The above example includes multiple predicates and subqueries within subqueries. This example answers the business question "Which employees in the same location as BLAKE earn less than the average salary?"

Let's look at the individual parts of this query and translate each into English.

```
SELECT * FROM EMP
 WHERE SAL <
           (SELECT AVG(SAL)       Subquery 1
            (FROM EMP)
 AND DEPTNO IN
     (SELECT DEPTNO FROM DEPT
      WHERE LOC =
                 (SELECT LOC FROM DEPT
                  WHERE DEPTNO =
                               (SELECT DEPTNO FROM EMP
                                WHERE ENAME = 'BLAKE')));
```

Subquery 1 translates to "the average salary in EMP." So the query now looks like this:

```
SELECT * FROM EMP
WHERE SAL < (the average salary in EMP)
AND DEPTNO IN (a list of DEPTNOs)
```

The list of DEPTNO values comes from subqueries 2, 3, and 4.

```
SELECT * FROM EMP
 WHERE SAL <
          (SELECT AVG(SAL)
           (FROM EMP)
 AND DEPTNO IN
     (SELECT DEPTNO FROM DEPT ─┐      Subquery 4
      WHERE LOC =              ┘
                (SELECT LOC FROM DEPT ─┐ Subquery 3
                 WHERE DEPTNO =        ┘
                              (SELECT DEPTNO FROM EMP    ─┐Subquery
                               WHERE ENAME = 'BLAKE')));─┘    2
```

With subqueries 2 through 4, you have a subquery (2) within a subquery (3) within a subquery (4). These subqueries are "nested."

```
Subquery 2, (SELECT ENAME FROM EMP

WHERE ENAME = 'BLAKE')
```

is computed next because it is the innermost subquery. This translates to "Blake's department number."

Subquery 3 is computed next because it is at the next level of parentheses. It now looks like:

```
SELECT LOC FROM DEPT
WHERE DEPTNO = (Blake's department number)
```

This translates to "The location with the same department number as Blake."

Subquery 4 now looks like:

```
SELECT DEPTNO FROM DEPT
WHERE LOC = (The location with the same department as Blake)
```

This translates to "Department numbers with the same location as Blake's department number."

The translation of the entire query is:

```
SELECT * FROM EMP
 WHERE SAL < (the average salary in EMP)
 AND DEPTNO IN (the list of DEPTNO values with the same
 location as Blake's department number)
```

This answers the original business request, "Which employees in the same location as Blake earn less than the average salary?"

ANY AND ALL

There is one important rule to keep in mind when using subqueries: The left side of a predicate requires a matching result from the subquery on the right.

For example, if the predicate involves a logical operator, a single value must be returned by the subquery:

```
number > (subquery returning a single number)

string = (subquery returning a single character string)
```

A different set of rules applies for the IN operator when used with a subquery. It works if the subquery returns one or more values. It even accepts no values (a NULL result), meaning the logical condition is false, and that particular row is not retrieved for the result.

Here are two examples:

```
number IN > (subquery returning a list of numbers)

string IN = (subquery returning a list of character strings)
```

But what if you use an operator such as > that only accepts single-value results from a subquery, and what if the subquery returns multiple results? An error message appears.

Luckily, SQL has a feature to allow multiple values returned by the subquery to be processed by a predicate that is designed to evaluate single values. Suppose you want to know who earns more than Smith does:

```
SELECT * FROM EMP
WHERE SAL >
      (SELECT SAL FROM EMP
       WHERE ENAME = 'SMITH');
```

If you are sure that there is only one SMITH in the EMP table, this query works. The subquery returns one single value, which is evaluated by a logical predicate expecting one single value.

But if there are two or more SMITHs in the EMP table, the subquery returns a list of numbers—one for each in row in EMP with an ENAME value of Smith. The query fails because the syntax

```
number > (list of numbers)
```

is incorrect.

SQL allows us to avoid failed queries of this type. You can use the SQL keyword **ANY** (compares a value to each value returned by a subquery) in this manner:

```
number > ANY (list of numbers)
```

The above expression is true, if the number on the left is greater than any one number in the list. The meaning of > ANY is "greater than at least one of those in the list."

ANY works with other logical predicates involving =, <, etc.

Another SQL feature used to handle multiple subquery results is **ALL** (compares a value to every value returned by a subquery).

It is used in this manner:

```
number > ALL (subquery returning a list of numbers)

string > ALL (subquery returning a list of character strings)
```

The first predicate above is true if the number on the left is greater than every number in the list. If the list is empty, the predicate is also true.

Any of the other logical operators, such as <>, >=, etc., work with ALL.

Be careful when using the logical operator = (equal) with ALL. Suppose the list returned by a subquery contains only one value, or contains the same value repeated more than once such as (5, 5, 5). The predicate:

```
number = ALL (list)
```

is true or false, depending on the value of the number on the left.

If the list has any duplicate values, such as (5, 5, 6, 5), then the predicate:

```
number = ALL (list)
```

is false because the number on the left cannot be equal to both 5 and 6 at the same time.

CORRELATED SUBQUERIES

When you use a regular subquery, it is executed first, and temporary results are held in the RDBMS's memory. The condition in the main query is checked against the result of the subquery. Rows are retrieved if they match the condition:

```
        WHERE SAL <
                  (SELECT AVG(SAL)...)

              |                |
        Main query         Subquery
        predicate          results
                               |
Row 1 SAL < A ----------------'    The same result is
Row 2 SAL < A ----------------'    checked against each
...
Row n SAL < A ----------------'    row of the table
```

A second type of subquery available in SQL is called the **correlated subquery**. In a correlated subquery, a value from the main query is passed to the subquery in order for the subquery to be executed.

Just as with regular subqueries, the result of a correlated subquery is used to evaluate the main query predicate, and retrieve rows for display. But with correlated subqueries, a new result is produced for each row of the table that is evaluated.

For example, suppose you want to answer the business question "Which people earn less than the average salary for everyone in the same job title as he or she is in?"

This translates into SQL as:

```
SELECT * FROM EMP
WHERE SAL < (AVG(SAL) for the same JOB value as contained
             in the row of the table being evaluated)
```

A correlated subquery computes the AVG(SAL), but not for all rows. The subquery needs to know which rows have the same JOB value as the row of the table being evaluated in the main query.

If the row in the table has a job value of CLERK, CLERK is passed to the subquery so it can compute AVG(SAL) for all rows with a JOB value of CLERK.

The next row of the table might contain a job value of MANAGER. This value would need to be passed to the subquery so it could compute AVG(SAL) for all rows with a JOB value of MANAGER.

How are these values passed to the subquery?

Correlated subqueries are carried out in SQL with **table labels** (also known as correlation names) and **correlated references**.

A table label is added to the table names in the main query and the subquery. The label may consist of one or more characters, and is separated from the table name by at least one space:

```
SELECT* FROM EMP MAIN   —— table label
WHERE SAL <
      (SELECT AVG(SAL)
       FROM EMP SUB ...);
                 |
                 |________________ table label
```

Here is how table labels are used to construct the query for the question "Which people earn less than the average salary for everyone in the same job title as he or she is in?" EMP is given the table label MAIN in the main query, and SUB in the subquery.

A correlated reference is added to the WHERE clause of the subquery to link the subquery with a value or values in the row being evaluated in the main query table. It usually takes the form:

```
WHERE SUB.<column_name> = MAIN.<column_name>
```

MAIN and SUB are the table labels of the tables in the main query and the subquery:

```
SELECT* FROM EMP MAIN
WHERE SAL <
      (SELECT AVG(SAL)
       FROM EMP       ...);
       WHERE SUB.JOB = MAIN.JOB);
             |_____________|
            correlated reference
```

Here is the completed query for "Which people earn less than the average salary for everyone in the same job title that he or she is in?"

The JOB value from the main query is passed to the subquery to produce the subquery's result:

```
      WHERE SAL <
                 (SELECT AVG(SAL)...)
                  FROM EMP SUB
                  WHERE SUB.JOB= MAIN.JOB);
            |                 |
       Main query          Subquery
       predicate           results
                              |
Row 1 SAL < A ————————————————|    Subquery results for
Row 2 SAL < B ————————————————|    each row are checked
...                                against the main
Row n SAL < C ————————————————|    query predicate.
```

When you use a correlated subquery, the subquery is executed for each row chosen in the main query.

To determine if the main query predicate is true or false, each row chosen by the main query is checked against the result of the subquery for that row.

EXISTS AND NOT EXISTS

A useful feature of SQL with correlated subqueries is the EXISTS predicate. The logical expression EXISTS (subquery) is TRUE if the subquery returns at least one row. It is FALSE if the subquery does not.

You use EXISTS in the WHERE clause in this way:

```
WHERE EXISTS (subquery)
```

Let's see how EXISTS can be used in a query.

Suppose you would like to list the departments from the DEPT table that have employees who earn commission.

This query lists those departments:

```
SELECT * FROM DEPT D
WHERE EXISTS
        (SELECT * FROM EMP E
         WHERE E.DEPTNO = D.DEPTNO
         AND COMM IS NOT NULL);
```

The main query retrieves rows from the DEPT table, using the table label or correlation name D.

The subquery chooses rows from the EMP table with non-NULL commission values and that have the same DEPTNO value as the DEPT row in the main query:

```
SELECT * FROM DEPT D  ──────────┐
WHERE EXISTS     ──true ┐      DEPTNO value
                        │        │
  (SELECT * FROM EMP E           │
   WHERE E.DEPTNO = D.DEPTNO  ───┘
   AND COMM IS NOT NULL);
```

If the row is selected by the subquery, then EXISTS (subquery) is true. Then the row from DEPT with the same DEPTNO value as the row from EMP chosen by the subquery is displayed.

The SELECT * format is adequate for the subquery because no temporary result is passed by the correlated subquery to the main query.

The negative of EXISTS is NOT EXISTS. It is used in the same manner as EXISTS:

```
WHERE NOT EXISTS (subquery)
```

Use NOT EXISTS to make sure that tables are properly loaded and refer to valid data:

```
SELECT * FROM EMP E
WHERE NOT EXISTS
       (SELECT *
        FROM DEPT D
        WHERE D.DEPTNO = E.DEPTNO);
```

This query displays any row in the EMP table that has an invalid DEPTNO value. A row is retrieved by the main query if there is a DEPTNO value in EMP (E.DEPTNO in the subquery) that does not exist among the DEPTNO values in DEPT (D.DEPTNO).

Complex queries, subqueries, and correlated subqueries are powerful tools.

However, many of these types of queries take a long time to run, even on the largest computer. Therefore, test your query with a small subset of data. This allows you to:

- Make sure your query does what you think it should do, and
- Estimate how long it will run with a larger amount of data

In this chapter, you learned how to:

- Define subqueries and use them in complex queries
- Identify the SQL features ANY and ALL, which are used with multiple subquery results
- Perform correlated subqueries with the components table labels and correlated references
- Employ the SQL features EXISTS and NOT EXISTS with correlated subqueries

Now let's look at some exercises to reinforce these skills.

Workshop Exercises

Advanced Subqueries

Now that you have learned about advanced subqueries, you can practice using them. In this section, you will practice the following concepts:

1. The use of ANY and ALL
2. The use of correlated subqueries
3. The use of EXISTS

Exercise 4.1

The ANY and ALL operators allow you to use a variety of logical predicates with subqueries that return more than a single value. Show clerks whose salary is greater than those of salespeople in the EMP table. List EMPNO, ENAME, JOB, and SAL.

RESULT TABLE:

```
EMPNO   ENAME    JOB      SAL
-----   ------   -----   -----
 7934   MILLER   CLERK    1300
```

Write your answer here:

Exercise 4.2

Show all employees whose salaries are higher than the salaries of every manager. Use the same format of results as in Exercise 4.1.

RESULT TABLE:

```
EMPNO   ENAME   JOB         SAL
-----   -----   ---------   ----
 7788   SCOTT   ANALYST     3000
 7839   KING    PRESIDENT   5000
 7902   FORD    ANALYST     3000
```

Write your answer here:

____

____

____

____

____

____

Exercise 4.3

Let's try to convert the following query (which may use a variant of the IN predicate) to use either ANY or ALL. "Show me the employees in Department 20 who don't have jobs that are found in Department 10." Select EMPNO, ENAME, JOB, and DEPTNO.

RESULT TABLE:

EMPNO	ENAME	JOB	DEPTNO
7788	SCOTT	ANALYST	20
7902	FORD	ANALYST	20

Write your answer here:

____

____

____

____

____

____

Exercise 4.4

A more complicated form of subquery is the correlated subquery, which you have already learned about. Show the employees (EMPNO, ENAME, DEPTNO, JOB, and SAL) who have the highest SAL in their department. (Hint: In the outer query, choose rows where the salary is equal to something from the same department.)

RESULT TABLE:

EMPNO	ENAME	DEPTNO	JOB	SAL
7698	BLAKE	30	MANAGER	2850
7788	SCOTT	20	ANALYST	3000
7839	KING	10	PRESIDENT	5000
7902	FORD	20	ANALYST	3000

Write your answer here:

____

____

____

____

____

____

Exercise 4.5

Try to solve this exercise with a correlated subquery as well. Show the departments (DEPTNO, DNAME, and LOC) that have at least four employees assigned. (Hint: In the outer query, choose rows where four compares to something from the same department.)

RESULT TABLE:

```
DEPTNO   DNAME      LOC
------   --------   -------
    20   RESEARCH   DALLAS
    30   SALES      CHICAGO
```

Write your answer here:

____

____

____

____

____

____

Exercise 4.6

Another predicate, EXISTS, is used with a correlation technique. Show the departments (DEPTNO, DNAME, and LOC) that have a manager or managers hired after one of the manager's subordinates. (Hint: In the outer query, choose rows where some join EXISTS involving the same department. Use the MGR to EMPNO linkage to find "managers.")

RESULT TABLE:

```
DEPTNO    DNAME         LOC
------    ----------    -----------
    10    ACCOUNTING    NEW YORK
    20    RESEARCH      DALLAS
    30    SALES         CHICAGO
```

Write your answer here:

___

___

___

___

___

___

Exercise 4.7

The negative of EXISTS is the NOT EXISTS predicate. It is particularly useful when some condition is missing (in which case a join wouldn't work). Show which employees with the JOB title 'MANAGER' have no employees reporting to them with the title 'ANALYST'. (Hint: In the outer query, choose rows where some subquery row does NOT EXIST involving the same MANAGER. Use the MGR to EMPNO linkage to find "subordinates.")

RESULT TABLE:

EMPNO	ENAME	JOB	MGR	HIREDATE	SAL	COMM	DEPTNO
7698	BLAKE	MANAGER	7839	01-MAY-81	2850		30
7782	CLARK	MANAGER	7839	09-JUN-81	2450		10

Write your answer here:

You have completed the exercises on advanced subqueries. To practice using advanced subqueries in a simulated SQL environment, choose Menu Item 3 from Exercise Disk 1.

Solutions to Workshop Exercises

Exercise 4.1 - Solution

```
SELECT EMPNO, ENAME, JOB, SAL
FROM EMP WHERE JOB = 'CLERK'
AND SAL > ANY
  (SELECT SAL FROM EMP
  WHERE JOB = 'SALESMAN');
```

Notes

This is a "trick question," used to reinforce the definition of ANY. If we had asked for "clerks whose salary is greater than any salesperson's salary," you might have been misled to use ANY. In English, "greater than any" usually means "higher than all possible values." The SQL ALL is what is implied by the English "greater than any," so be careful!

We've used ANY in our answer to select the clerks whose SAL is more than any one salesperson's SAL. When you use ANY, the predicate is compared to "at least one of those in the list." This could have been restated in SQL as:

```
... SAL > (SELECT MIN(SAL)...)
```

Exercise 4.2 - Solution

```
SELECT EMPNO, ENAME, JOB, SAL
FROM EMP WHERE
SAL > ALL
  (SELECT SAL FROM EMP
  WHERE JOB = 'MANAGER');
```

Notes

In this case, the format of the question does not mislead. We ask for employees whose SAL is greater than every manager's SAL. This is the definition of the ALL operator. The SQL alternative for this query is:

```
... SAL > (SELECT MAX(SAL)...)
```

Exercise 4.3 - Solution

```
SELECT EMPNO, ENAME, JOB, DEPTNO
FROM EMP WHERE DEPTNO = 20
AND JOB <> ALL
  (SELECT JOB FROM EMP
  WHERE DEPTNO = 10);
```

Notes

Usually SQL users would choose the regular format of the answer with the NOT IN predicate:

```
AND JOB NOT IN (SELECT JOB FROM EMP...)
```

Our answer with JOB < > ALL is equivalent. The following shows both the positive and negative IN predicates and the ANY/ALL equivalents:

```
JOB IN (subquery) <==> JOB = ANY (subquery)
JOB NOT IN (subquery) <==> JOB < > ALL (subquery)
```

Exercise 4.4 - Solution

```
SELECT EMPNO, ENAME, DEPTNO, JOB, SAL
FROM EMP O
WHERE SAL =
  (SELECT MAX(SAL)
  FROM EMP I
  WHERE I.DEPTNO = O.DEPTNO);
```

Notes

Unlike the regular subquery in the previous exercises, a correlated subquery has some value in the outer query row that is passed to the subquery in order for the subquery to run. The subquery is executed repeatedly.

In our answer, which value from the outer query is passed to the inner query?

It is the O.DEPTNO value, the outer query row's DEPTNO value. The inner query uses it to choose rows from which it develops a MAX(SAL) value to pass back to the outer query. The outer query then uses the MAX(SAL) value calculated for each outer row's own department to help choose outer rows.

You could have chosen any name for the table labels. We chose O and I to represent Outer and Inner queries. The inner query does not need a table label at all. The subquery needs to know which rows have the same JOB had by the outer row. If the outer row is "Clerk," then the subquery needs to know "CLERK" to compute AVG(SAL) for all rows having "Clerk," or WHERE JOB = 'Clerk'.

Exercise 4.5 - Solution

```
SELECT DEPTNO, DNAME, LOC
FROM DEPT D
WHERE 4 <=
  (SELECT COUNT(*)
  FROM EMP E
  WHERE E.DEPTNO = D.DEPTNO);
```

Notes

Again, the D.DEPTNO value is passed to the inner query for each row in the outer query. The inner query uses that value to choose a set of inner rows with that DEPTNO. It then counts rows from that department, returning a value, COUNT(*), to the outer query. If the number is four or more, then the outer row is selected.

This same result also can be obtained without using a subquery. In the following example, a join is used with grouping:

```
SELECT D.DEPTNO, D.DNAME, D.LOC
FROM DEPT D, EMP E
WHERE E.DEPTNO = D.DEPTNO
GROUP BY D.DEPTNO, D.DNAME, D.LOC
HAVING COUNT(*) >= 4;
```

A few comments may be helpful at this point. All three columns, DEPTNO, DNAME, and LOC, change together for each row in the DEPT table, so we can group by all three as easily as grouping by just DEPTNO. This allows us to use the three columns in our SELECT clause with grouping.

Exercise 4.6 - Solution

```
SELECT DEPTNO, DNAME, LOC
FROM DEPT D
WHERE EXISTS
  (SELECT M.*
  FROM EMP M, EMP E
  WHERE M.EMPNO = E.MGR
  AND M.DEPTNO = D.DEPTNO
  AND M.HIREDATE > E.HIREDATE);
```

Notes

The D.DEPTNO value from the outer row is passed to the inner query. The outer row is chosen if the EXISTS predicate returns a TRUE value. This will occur if the subquery finds at least one row matching its conditions.

Let's go over each section of the subquery:

SELECT M.* We can request any part of the inner result in the SELECT clause because it is not returned to the outer query; only TRUE or FALSE is returned. Note that an all NULL result is TRUE.

FROM EMP M, EMP E The inner query is a join of the WHERE M.EMPNO = E.MGR EMP table to itself, first as Manager (M) and then as Employee (E). The manager's EMPNO must be found in an Employee's MGR column in order to join.

AND M.DEPTNO = D.DEPTNO This is the correlation variable. It requires that the Manager be from the outer row's department.

AND M.HIREDATE > E.HIREDATE Finally we check that the Manager's date of hire is after the Employee's.

This particular query could be performed other ways, without the EXISTS predicate. One other solution is to use a triple join.

Exercise 4.7 - Solution

```
SELECT *
FROM EMP M
WHERE M.JOB = 'MANAGER'
AND NOT EXISTS
  (SELECT S.*
  FROM EMP S
  WHERE M.EMPNO = S.MGR
  AND S.JOB = 'ANALYST');
```

Notes

In this query, first all of the outer rows are chosen to be "MANAGER" rows. The M.EMPNO value from the Manager outer row is passed to the subquery as the correlation variable.

NOT EXISTS returns a TRUE value if no match is found. We are saying, "I hope it is not true that something exists."

In the subquery we are trying to find any row of a subordinate "S" that is an "ANALYST." The subordinates of our Manager row are:

```
SELECT S.* FROM EMP S WHERE M.EMPNO = S.MGR
```

The correlated outer Manager number M.EMPNO must be in subordinate's MGR column, S.MGR. If anyone is also an ANALYST:

```
AND S.JOB = 'ANALYST'
```

then we have a TRUE for the subquery. NOT EXISTS makes it FALSE, so we don't choose the manager for that outer row. If NO INNER row is a subordinate ANALYST, the inner query returns FALSE, and the NOT EXISTS makes it TRUE; that is one of the managers we are seeking.

5

Advanced Use of Joins

In this chapter you will be introduced to the substitution of joins for subqueries. You will see how joins can be used with control tables, views, and the UNION operator.

JOIN REVIEW

Let's review the relational join operation and compare it to the use of subqueries.

When the relational database management system (RDBMS) joins two tables, it places a row of the first table beside a row of the second table:

```
       Row from table A                       Row from table B

 | A1 | A2 | A3          |          | B1 | B2      | B3     | B4 |
```

The system then displays each row of the result table according to your SQL query. Suppose your SELECT clause was:

```
SELECT B2, B1, A3, B4.
```

A1	A2	A3

B1	B2	B3	B4

Each row of the table resulting from the join has this structure:

B2	B1	A3	B4

To join two tables, you specify the tables in the FROM clause, separated by commas. Each table name may be followed by aliases (table labels) such as TE and TD, shown in the query below:

```
SELECT EMPNO, DNAME, TD.DEPTNO
FROM EMP TE, DEPT TD
WHERE TE.DEPTNO = TD.DEPTNO;
```

In this example, TE and TD are the aliases for the EMP and DEPT tables, respectively. You specify the table label, or alias, by leaving at least one space after the table name before typing the alias.

Where the query requires that a table name be used to qualify a column name, use the alias in place of the entire table name:

```
SELECT EMPNO, DNAME, TD.DEPTNO
FROM EMP TE, DEPT TD
WHERE TE.DEPTNO = TD.DEPTNO;
```

Remember, always avoid ambiguity when the tables being joined have identical column names in them. Specify one or the other table as its source by qualifying the column name with the table name, or alias, followed by a period. (TD.DEPTNO is an example of a qualified table name.)

The SELECT clause in our example query could be written as:

```
SELECT EMPNO, DNAME, DEPT.DEPTNO
```

This tells the RDBMS which DEPTNO column to use, the one from the EMP table or the one from the DEPT table. It doesn't matter whether the qualified column name uses the table name or its alias. The same is true for the qualified column names in the WHERE clause.

In a join query such as our example, the predicate (logical condition):

```
TE.DEPTNO = TD.DEPTNO
```

is called the join predicate. A join predicate provides a logical link that joins rows of one table with rows of the other table. These rows are joined whenever the DEPTNO column value in TE matches the DEPTNO column value in TD.

It's a good idea to list the join predicate in the WHERE clause of your join query. This way you won't forget it.

If tables are matched on values in two columns, include two predicates connected by AND:

```
SELECT E.EMPNO, B.ENAME, E.DEPTNO
FROM EMP E, BONUS B
WHERE E.ENAME = B.ENAME
AND E.JOB = B.JOB
AND DEPTNO IN (10, 20);
```

This query finds employees who are in Departments 10 and 20 and who are getting a bonus. Two columns are used to join these tables. Therefore, the two highlighted predicates are needed for the join query.

What happens if you leave off the join predicate?

```
SELECT EMPNO, DNAME, TD.DEPTNO
FROM EMP TE, DEPT TD;
```

The result is called a cartesian product. Cartesian products are usually worthless. For example, this one combines each row in TE in turn to each row in TD!

SUBSTITUTING JOINS FOR SUBQUERIES

When a subquery supplies a column value or list of values to a predicate in the main query, the main query may be converted to a join without a subquery.

Here is an example of a main query and a subquery that provides a list of employees who work in Dallas:

```
SELECT ENAME FROM EMP
WHERE DEPTNO IN
      (SELECT DEPTNO FROM DEPT
      WHERE LOC = 'DALLAS');
```

The main query retrieves rows from the EMP table. The subquery is used in this situation because the location DALLAS is in another table, DEPT.

You could join the EMP and DEPT tables because they both contain a DEPTNO column:

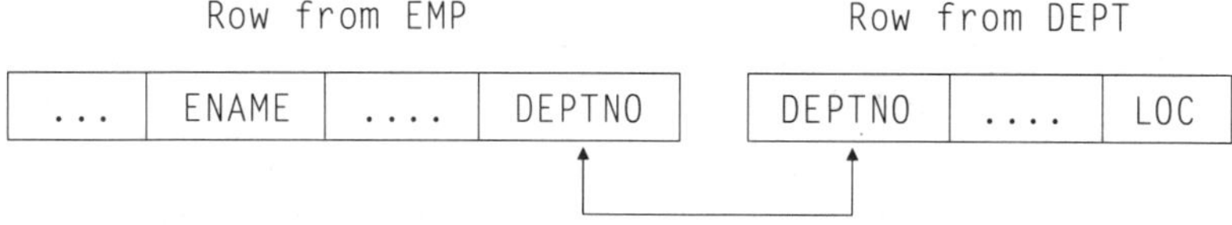

You can transform the subquery:

```
SELECT ENAME FROM EMP
WHERE DEPTNO IN
      (SELECT DEPTNO FROM DEPT
      WHERE LOC = 'DALLAS');
```

into a join:

```
SELECT ENAME FROM EMP E, DEPT D
WHERE E.DEPTNO = D.DEPTNO
AND D.LOC = 'DALLAS';
```

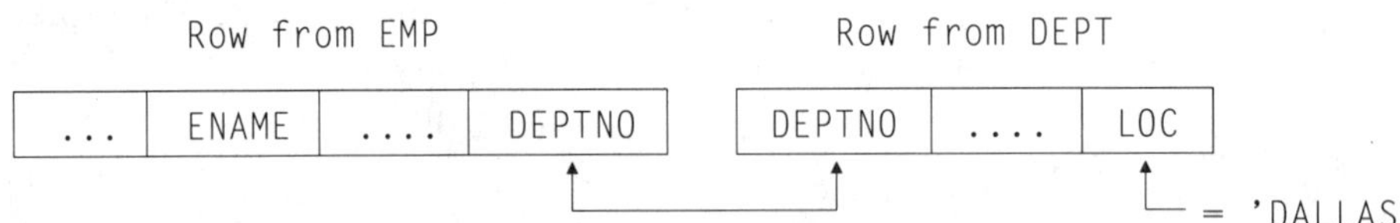

The result of the join is the same as the result of the subquery because the same column value (ENAME) is selected in both queries. In the query using a subquery, the WHERE clause predicate includes the subquery to find the DEPTNO values for those departments located in Dallas. ENAME values from the EMP table are then displayed, if the row they are in has a DEPTNO value matching one of those retrieved by the subquery.

In the join query, rows from both the EMP and DEPT tables are joined by the predicate E.DEPTNO = D.DEPTNO. ENAME values from the joined rows are displayed if the LOC values are 'DALLAS.' Because the ENAME value in the joined rows came from the EMP table, the result is the same as that for the query using the subquery.

Example

Suppose you want a list of the employees who work for the manager named Clark. The subquery that carries out this task is:

```
SELECT ENAME FROM EMP
WHERE MGR =
      (SELECT EMPNO FROM EMP
       WHERE ENAME = 'CLARK'
       AND JOB = 'MGR');
```

How could you use a join to carry out the same task?

Remember that a table can be joined to itself. Because the MGR column contains employee numbers of managers, the EMP table can be joined to itself using the MGR and EMPNO columns:

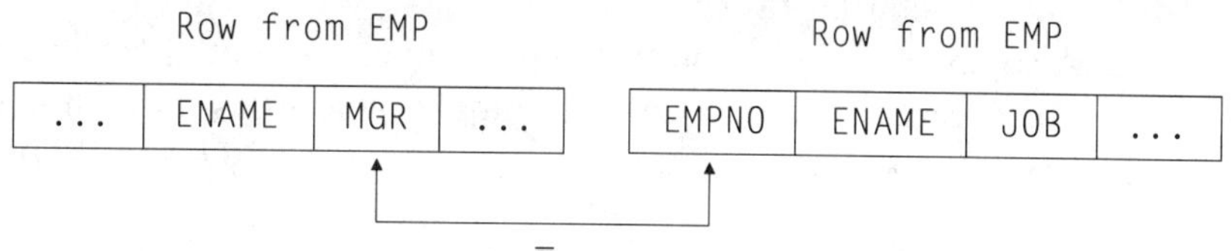

The subquery:

```
SELECT ENAME FROM EMP
WHERE MGR =
      (SELECT EMPNO FROM EMP
       WHERE ENAME = 'CLARK'
       AND JOB = 'MGR');
```

can be converted to the join:

```
SELECT E.ENAME FROM EMP E, EMP M
WHERE E.MGR = M.EMPNO
AND M.ENAME = 'CLARK'
AND M.JOB = 'MANAGER';
```

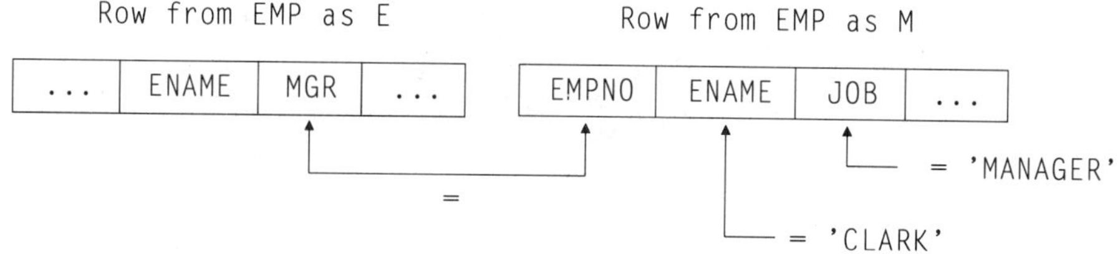

The result is the same because the same column value (ENAME) is selected by both queries. In the query using a subquery, both the main query and the subquery select values from the EMP table. ENAME values are selected if the row they are in has a MGR value that is identical for the EMPNO value selected by the subquery. The subquery selects Clark's EMPNO.

The join query connects each row from the EMP (as E) table to each row from the same table (as M) having a MGR value equal to the EMPNO in that particular row of E. In other words, employees' rows are joined to their managers' rows.

ENAME from EMP (as E) is displayed if the manager's name is Clark. Here (M.ENAME = 'CLARK') and the manager's JOB is 'MANAGER.' The last predicate ensures that Clark is, indeed, a manager.

Each RDBMS has different strategies for producing the results of joins. It is likely that one of these strategies runs faster than a corresponding subquery. Therefore, for large tables of data, run both a subquery and its equivalent join to determine which runs faster.

Also, indexes will improve the performance of both joins and subqueries.

For optimal performance, you may be able to avoid both the join and the subquery, if you can avoid the predicate value directly (as in WHERE DEPTNO = 20).

Be careful. Some joins may produce different answers from what seems to be the equivalent subquery. Sometimes multiple rows are joined when multiple occurrences of the same value exist. For example:

```
SELECT DNAME FROM DEPT
WHERE DEPTNO IN
      (SELECT DEPTNO FROM EMP
      WHERE JOB = 'CLERK';
```

The subquery returns four values in its list:

```
SELECT DNAME FROM DEPT
WHERE DEPTNO IN (20, 20, 30, 10);
```

which produces a three-row result:

```
DNAME
----------
ACCOUNTING
RESEARCH
SALES
```

In contrast to the subquery approach, the join version:

```
SELECT DNAME FROM DEPT D, EMP E
WHERE D.DEPTNO = E.DEPTNO
AND E.JOB = 'CLERK';
```

produces a four-row result:

```
DNAME
----------
ACCOUNTING
RESEARCH
RESEARCH
SALES
```

If you use the DISTINCT operator, you can eliminate duplicates. The DISTINCT operator tests for duplicate rows. But this approach requires extra processing time by the RDBMS:

```
SELECT DISTINCT DNAME FROM DEPT D, EMP E
WHERE D.DEPTNO = E.DEPTNO
AND E.JOB = 'CLERK';
```

This produces the desired three-row result. DISTINCT causes the result to be sorted:

```
DNAME
----------
ACCOUNTING
RESEARCH
SALES
```

Why does the subquery produce a three-row result, but the join produces a four-row result?

The DEPT table contains only four rows, one for each department. Each DNAME value and DEPTNO value in DEPT is distinct. Each row is compared against the list of department numbers (20, 20, 30, 10) retrieved by the subquery.

The first row of DEPT contains a DEPTNO value of 10 and a DNAME value of ACCOUNTING. The DEPTNO value of 10 is in the list. Therefore, the DNAME value of ACCOUNTING is displayed.

This process continues for each of the four rows. Three of the four rows have DEPTNOs that match the list. Therefore, the DNAMEs for these rows are displayed. No duplicates are displayed, because there are no duplicate values of DNAME in DEPT.

When the join is performed, each row of DEPT is joined to the row in EMP that has the same DEPTNO value and the JOB value 'CLERK.' Because there are two clerks in Department 20 (Research), there are two joined rows containing the DEPTNO value 20 and the job value 'CLERK,' one for Smith and one for Adams.

When the DNAME values from the joined rows are displayed, then RESEARCH is displayed twice.

Some subqueries cannot be converted directly into joins. Multiple predicates involving subqueries may prevent such conversions.

Subqueries involving aggregate functions or GROUP BY cannot be directly converted to joins, for example:

```
SELECT ENAME FROM EMP
WHERE SAL >
      (SELECT AVG(SAL) FROM EMP);
```

You can, however, store the result of an aggregate function in a temporary table and perform a join using that table. Here's an example.

Suppose the result of the subquery SELECT:

```
SELECT AVG(SAL) FROM EMP;
```

is stored in a column called AVG_SAL in a temporary table called TEMP.

You can join each row of EMP to TEMP. We don't need a join predicate in this case, because the single row in TEMP will be joined to each row in EMP (like a cartesian product).

```
     Each row from EMP          Single row from TEMP

 ---------------------------     -------------
 | ....... | ENAME  | SAL  |     |  AVG_SAL  |
 ---------------------------     -------------
```

Here is the join query that converts the subquery to a join using the temporary table TEMP:

```
SELECT ENAME
FROM EMP, TEMP
WHERE SAL > AVG_SAL;
```

Notice that it is not necessary to qualify column names, because none of them is contained in both tables.

Use this query and subquery to determine which employees in our company earn less salary and commission than the average salary and commission earned by salespeople:

```
SELECT ENAME FROM EMP
WHERE SAL + COMM <
      (SELECT AVG(SAL + COMM)
      WHERE JOB = 'SALESMAN');
```

The last example showed how to convert a subquery containing an aggregate function:

```
SELECT ENAME FROM EMP WHERE SAL >
      (SELECT AVG(SAL) FROM EMP);
```

into a join with a temporary table:

```
SELECT ENAME FROM EMP, TEMP
WHERE SAL> AVG_SAL;
```

It is possible to aggregate results using data from two tables that are joined together. For example, suppose you want to print a report about the departments contained in the EMP table. For each department, you want to list the department name, the number of employees in the department, and the average salary of that department.

This requires joining the DEPT and EMP tables, and using aggregate functions on the joined rows:

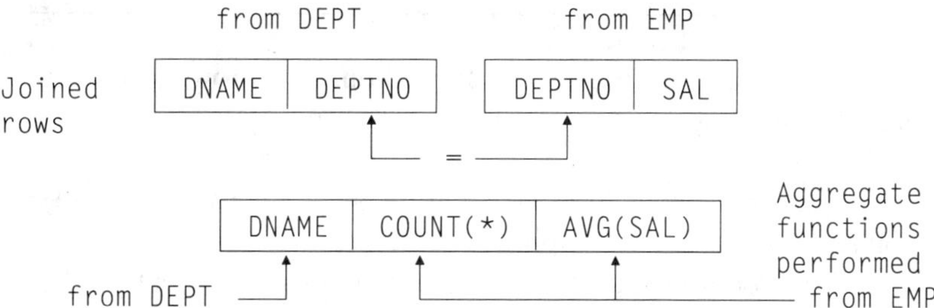

Now build the query. The SELECT clause is:

```
SELECT D.DNAME, COUNT(*), AVG(E.SAL)
```

Qualify the DNAME and SAL names because they are contained in both the DEPT and EMP tables. Assign the DEPT table the label D and the EMP table the label E.

The FROM clause is next:

```
FROM DEPT D, EMP E
```

Add the join predicate to join rows from the two tables:

```
WHERE D.DEPTNO = E.DEPTNO
```

Finally, form groups of each DNAME value:

```
GROUP BY D.DNAME;
```

Qualify DNAME with a table label because it is in both tables.

Here is the completed query:

```
SELECT D.DNAME, COUNT(*), AVG(E.SAL)
FROM DEPT D, EMP E
WHERE D.DEPTNO = E.DEPTNO
GROUP BY D.DNAME;
```

Here are the results:

```
DNAME           COUNT(*)  AVG(E.SAL)
--------------  --------  ----------
ACCOUNTING             3     2916.67
RESEARCH               5        2175
SALES                  6     1566.67
```

Aggregate functions work as well on joined rows as they do on rows from a single table. You can develop a join and then aggregate rows as if they were from a single table.

Here is another example of using aggregate functions in conjunction with joins. In this case, no grouping is involved.

Suppose you want to count the number of different job titles and the number of different salary grades for employees who are managers or who work in Department 30.

You need to join the EMP and SALGRADE tables. You are interested in the JOB, SAL, and DEPTNO columns from the EMP table, and the GRADE, LOSAL, and HISAL columns from the SALGRADE table:

from EMP

JOB	SAL	DEPTNO

from SALGRADE

GRADE	LOSAL	HISAL

To answer your business question, you need to count the distinct JOB values in EMP and the distinct GRADE values in SALGRADE. Look at rows where the job value is 'MANAGER' or the DEPTNO value is 30. Here is the query:

```
SELECT
COUNT(DISTINCT E.JOB),       ──┐   aggregations
COUNT (DISTINCT S.GRADE)     ──┘
FROM EMP E, SALGRADE S
WHERE E.SAL BETWEEN S.LOSAL AND S.HISAL    ── join predicate
AND
(E.JOB = 'MANAGER' OR E.DEPTNO = 30);   ── additional predicates
```

Notice that the join predicate is in a different form than you may be used to. The join predicate uses the BETWEEN operator, rather than the = (equal to) operator.

The join produces these rows, before the aggregate functions are performed:

JOB	SAL	DEPTNO	GRADE	LOSAL	HISAL
CLERK	950	30	1	700	1200
SALESMAN	1250	30	2	1201	1400
SALESMAN	1250	30	2	1201	1400
SALESMAN	1600	30	3	1401	2000
SALESMAN	1500	30	3	1401	2000
MANAGER	2975	20	4	2001	3000
MANAGER	2850	30	4	2001	3000
MANAGER	2450	10	4	2001	3000

Can you count the distinct JOBs and GRADEs?

Once the aggregate functions are performed, you see these results:

from EMP　　　　from SALGRADE

COUNT(DISTINCT E.JOB)	COUNT(DISTINCT S.GRADE)
3	4

JOINS WITH CONTROL TABLES

Sometimes a report needs to be prepared in different sequences, and not all sequences can be derived directly from the columns of data.

For example, two executives may want a report on salaries by job title. But one needs the job titles alphabetically (a sequence that can come from the JOB column). The other needs job titles in another sequence.

A useful technique to solve the problem of preparing reports in different sequences is to use a control table. The control table may be joined to the regular table. The control table provides other columns needed to sequence the query.

Here's an example. The first executive needs JOB values shown in two categories: managerial and administrative. The second executive wants job titles shown in this manner: managerial, nonmanagerial exempt, and clerical/administrative. First, produce a control table, CTL1:

```
EXEC  TC  TYPE            SEQ  JOB
----  --  --------------  ---  -----------
1      1  MANAGERIAL        1  PRESIDENT
1      1  MANAGERIAL        2  MANAGER
1      2  ADMINISTRATIVE    3  ANALYST
1      2  ADMINISTRATIVE    4  SALESMAN
1      2  ADMINISTRATIVE    5  CLERK
2      1  MANAGERIAL        1  PRESIDENT
2      1  MANAGERIAL        2  MANAGER
2      2  NON-MAN/EXEMPT    3  ANALYST
2      2  NON-MAN/EXEMPT    4  SALESMAN
2      3  CLERICAL/ADMIN    5  CLERK
```

The control table can be joined to the EMP table by matching on the JOB column, a column contained in both tables. When the join is performed, all of the data in CTL1 become available to every row with that same job.

When a join is performed, you need to use a predicate to specify which executive (EXEC) is involved, Executive 1 or 2.

The TC (type code) corresponds to the TYPE column and allows users to sort by TC to maintain the sequence of TYPEs requested by the executive for each type. If TC is not available, sorting by TYPE results in ADMINISTRATIVE types coming before MANAGERIAL.

The SEQ column in the control table represents the order in which the executive wants to see the jobs displayed. The control table is joined to the EMP table to display information in the required order.

Remember that Executive 2 wants JOB values shown in this order: managerial, nonmanagerial exempt, and clerical/ administrative.

This query lists the data in order:

```
SELECT C.TC, C.TYPE, C.SEQ, E.JOB, E.SAL
FROM CTL1 C, EMP E
WHERE C.JOB = E.JOB      ←  join by matching JOB
AND C.EXEC = 2           ←  choose EXEC 2
ORDER BY C.TC, C.SEQ;    ←  maintain sequence
```

Here are the results:

```
     TC TYPE                SEQ JOB                SAL
------- -------------- ------- ------------ -------
      1 MANAGERIAL            1 PRESIDENT          5000
      1 MANAGERIAL            2 MANAGER            2975
      1 MANAGERIAL            2 MANAGER            2850
      1 MANAGERIAL            2 MANAGER            2450
      2 NON-MAN/EXEMPT        3 ANALYST            3000
      2 NON-MAN/EXEMPT        3 ANALYST            3000
      2 NON-MAN/EXEMPT        4 SALESMAN           1600
      2 NON-MAN/EXEMPT        4 SALESMAN           1250
      2 NON-MAN/EXEMPT        4 SALESMAN           1250
      2 NON-MAN/EXEMPT        4 SALESMAN           1500
      3 CLERICAL/ADMIN        5 CLERK               800
      3 CLERICAL/ADMIN        5 CLERK               950
      3 CLERICAL/ADMIN        5 CLERK              1100
      3 CLERICAL/ADMIN        5 CLERK              1300
```

Within the managerial type (TC = 1), presidents are listed first and managers second. Within the nonmanagerial/exempt type (TC = 2), analysts are listed first and only salespeople second. Within the clerical/administrative type (TC = 3), clerks are listed.

JOINS WITH SUBQUERIES

Subqueries can be used with joins and joins can be used with subqueries. These complex queries may not run quickly with larger tables. Remember this query from earlier in the chapter:

```
SELECT D.DNAME, COUNT(*), AVG(E.SAL)
FROM DEPT D, EMP E
WHERE D.DEPTNO = E.DEPTNO
GROUP BY D.DNAME;
```

The following example adds a subquery to this join. The subquery limits the aggregated rows to those matching employees in the BONUS table:

```
SELECT D.DNAME, COUNT(*), AVG(E.SAL)
FROM DEPT D, EMP E
WHERE D.DEPTNO = E.DEPTNO
AND E.ENAME IN
    (SELECT ENAME FROM BONUS)
GROUP BY D.DNAME;
```

and produces:

```
DNAME           COUNT(*)  AVG(E.SAL)
--------------  --------  ----------
RESEARCH               2      1887.5
SALES                  3     1366.67
```

A join also may be used within a subquery. Here's how to list all departments without employees who are in line for a bonus:

```
SELECT * FROM DEPT D WHERE NOT EXISTS
       (SELECT E.*
        FROM EMP E, BONUS B
        WHERE E.ENAME = B.ENAME AND
        E.DEPTNO = D.DEPTNO)
```

The first two WHERE clause predicates in this subquery are:

`WHERE E.ENAME = B.ENAME`	—the join predicate for the subquery, linking its two tables together
`AND E.DEPTNO = D.DEPTNO)`	—the correlation variable linking the subquery to the main query

UNION

The joining of rows from two or more tables places the rows side by side. Another relational operation, UNION, stacks rows from different SELECT statements one under the other to form the results:

part of row from table A
part of row from table A
part of row from table B
part of row from table B
part of row from table B

UNION displays distinct rows returned by either of the queries it combines.

Each of the SELECT statements operated on by UNION can have a join, subquery, or GROUP BY, as well as other WHERE clause predicates.

The syntax of UNION is:

```
query-1 UNION query-2 ... [ORDER BY];
```

Each query may be any complete SELECT statement, but it may not contain an ORDER BY clause. An ORDER BY clause may be added at the end of the UNION operation.

Here's an example of how to use UNION. Suppose you want to display employees who receive a bonus or who have above-average salaries. Use UNION to accomplish this task:

```
SELECT E.EMPNO, E.ENAME                  ──┐
FROM EMP E, BONUS B                        │ — First query, a join
WHERE E.ENAME = B.ENAME                  ──┘

UNION

SELECT EMPNO, ENAME                      ──┐
FROM EMP WHERE SAL >                       │ — Second query, a
     (SELECT AVG(SAL) FROM EMP)          ──┘   subquery

ORDER BY 2;
```

The first query above is a join of two tables. The second query has a simple subquery. Note that the ORDER BY clause is placed last.

Here are the rules for UNION:

1. The number of expressions in each query must be equal.
2. The data types of corresponding expressions of each query must be compatible. Compatible means that, if the first expression is of a numeric data type, corresponding first expressions must also be of a numeric data type.
3. The column names of corresponding columns in the two queries do not have to be the same. Here is a valid SQL statement:

   ```
   SELECT SAL FROM EMP
   UNION
   SELECT COMM FROM BONUS;
   ```

4. Because of the possibility of corresponding column names in the queries being different, the optional ORDER BY clause after the last query must order by position, not by name. ORDER BY 1 is correct, ORDER BY E.EMPNO is not.

UNION eliminates duplicate rows of results. This means that, when all column values of two result rows match, one result row is dropped from the results table. For instance, you want to show all managers and all employees who are eligible for bonuses in addition to their salaries. Here is the query we can use:

```
SELECT ENAME, SAL FROM BONUS
UNION
SELECT ENAME, SAL FROM EMP WHERE JOB = 'MANAGER';
```

The individual results of each query are:

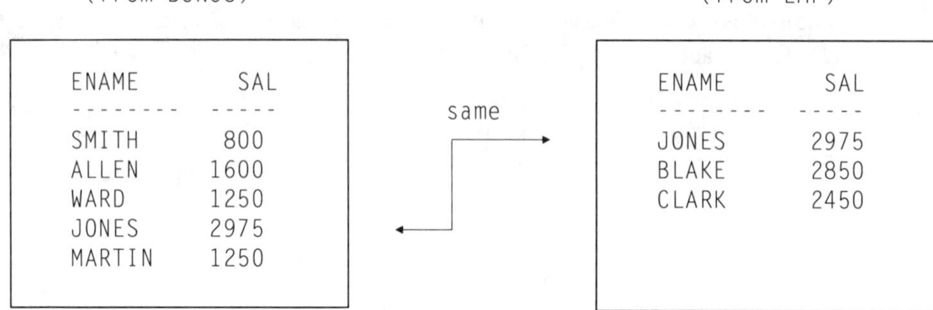

(from BONUS)

ENAME	SAL
SMITH	800
ALLEN	1600
WARD	1250
JONES	2975
MARTIN	1250

(from EMP)

ENAME	SAL
JONES	2975
BLAKE	2850
CLARK	2450

UNION combines the results of the individual queries and removes duplicate rows:

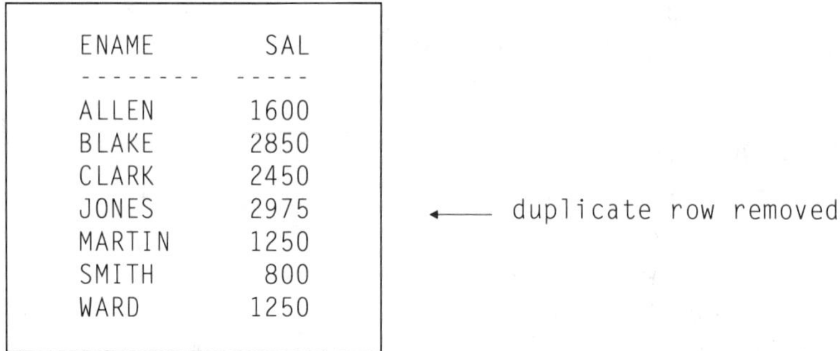

ENAME	SAL
ALLEN	1600
BLAKE	2850
CLARK	2450
JONES	2975
MARTIN	1250
SMITH	800
WARD	1250

Notice that the RDBMS sorts the results to find the duplicate row.

Let's take another look at a previous example.

This example displayed employees who receive a bonus or who have above-average salaries. Suppose you want to know which rows come from the first query (eligible for bonuses) and which come from the second (above-average salaries).

```
SELECT E.EMPNO, E.ENAME, 'GETTING BONUS'
FROM EMP E, BONUS B
WHERE E.ENAME = B.ENAME
UNION
SELECT EMPNO, ENAME, 'ABOVE AVERAGE SALARY'
FROM EMP WHERE SAL >
     (SELECT AVG(SAL) FROM EMP)
ORDER BY 2;
```

Here are the results:

```
  EMPNO  ENAME           'GETTING BONUS'
------- --------------  ---------------------
   7499  ALLEN           GETTING BONUS
   7698  BLAKE           ABOVE AVERAGE SALARY
   7782  CLARK           ABOVE AVERAGE SALARY
   7902  BLAKE           ABOVE AVERAGE SALARY
   7566  JONES           ABOVE AVERAGE SALARY
   7566  JONES           GETTING BONUS
   7839  KING            ABOVE AVERAGE SALARY
   7654  MARTIN          GETTING BONUS
   7788  SCOTT           ABOVE AVERAGE SALARY
   7369  SMITH           GETTING BONUS
   7521  WARD            GETTING BONUS
```

VIEWS WITH JOINS

If you frequently use certain complex queries, here is a shortcut that hides them in views.

Almost any feature of SQL may be used when a view is defined. (ORDER BY is an exception.)

You may even define views on top of other views. Also, most views may be joined to tables or other views.

You should know whether a view can be updated or is read-only.

For example, views defined on joins of multiple tables are read-only and may not have updates done through them.

UPDATE, INSERT, or DELETE cannot be performed through a read-only view.

In addition to limiting updates through a join view, views are also read-only if their definitions:

- Are themselves based on read-only views

or contain one of the following:

- DISTINCT
- GROUP BY
- HAVING
- Aggregate functions (like SUM)
- Subqueries based on the same table

Consider this join query:

```
SELECT EMPNO, ENAME, TD.DEPTNO, DNAME
FROM EMP TE, DEPT TD
WHERE TE.DEPTNO = TD.DEPTNO;
```

Embed it into a new view called EMP_DEPT as follows:

```
CREATE VIEW EMP_DEPT
  (EMPNO, ENAME, DEPTNO, DNAME) AS
SELECT EMPNO, ENAME, TD.DEPTNO, DNAME
FROM EMP TE, DEPT TD
WHERE TE.DEPTNO = TD.DEPTNO;
```

The view EMP_DEPT defines a join. You may perform that join by selecting from the view EMP_DEPT directly:

```
SELECT EMPNO, ENAME, DEPTNO, DNAME
FROM EMP_DEPT;
```

Any additional predicates may be added to the query upon the view. Suppose you need to know all employees in the SALES department:

```
SELECT EMPNO, ENAME, DEPTNO, DNAME
FROM EMP_DEPT;
WHERE DNAME = 'SALES';
```

This is equivalent to the following query:

```
SELECT EMPNO, ENAME, TD.DEPTNO, DNAME
FROM EMP TE, DEPT TD
WHERE (TE.DEPTNO = TD.DEPTNO) AND (DNAME = 'SALES');
```

The system adds the new predicate to the view definition's search conditions.

In this chapter, you learned how to:

- Substitute joins for subqueries
- Define aliases and join predicates
- Use joins with control tables and subqueries
- Stack rows of joined tables with the UNION operator
- Hide complex queries in views

Let's practice these topics with some workshop exercises.

Workshop Exercises

Advanced Use of Joins

In this section, you will practice the following concepts:

1. The use of joins
2. The use of cartesian products
3. The use of inequalities in the join predicate
4. Converting subqueries into joins

Exercise 5.1

Let's begin the lesson with a straightforward join. Show the employees, with their department information alongside. Sort the report by department number. Show DEPTNO, DNAME, LOC, EMPNO, ENAME, and JOB.

RESULT TABLE:

```
DEPTNO  DNAME       LOC       EMPNO  ENAME   JOB
------  ----------  --------  -----  -----   -------
    10  ACCOUNTING  NEW YORK   7782  CLARK   MANAGER
    10  ACCOUNTING  NEW YORK   7839  KING    PRESIDENT
    10  ACCOUNTING  NEW YORK   7934  MILLER  CLERK
    20  RESEARCH    DALLAS     7369  SMITH   CLERK
    20  RESEARCH    DALLAS     7902  FORD    ANALYST
    20  RESEARCH    DALLAS     7566  JONES   MANAGER
    20  RESEARCH    DALLAS     7876  ADAMS   CLERK
    20  RESEARCH    DALLAS     7788  SCOTT   ANALYST
    30  SALES       CHICAGO    7499  ALLEN   SALESMAN
    30  SALES       CHICAGO    7654  MARTIN  SALESMAN
    30  SALES       CHICAGO    7521  WARD    SALESMAN
    30  SALES       CHICAGO    7900  JAMES   CLERK
    30  SALES       CHICAGO    7844  TURNER  SALESMAN
    30  SALES       CHICAGO    7698  BLAKE   MANAGER
```

Write your answer here:

____

____

____

____

____

____

Exercise 5.2

Here's a slightly more difficult join. Show all the information in the BONUS table, plus the employees' EMPNO and HIREDATE columns added on the right. (Hint: Can you join using one column?)

RESULT TABLE:

```
ENAME    JOB        SAL   COMM   EMPNO   HIREDATE
------   --------   ----  ----   -----   ---------
ALLEN    SALESMAN   1600   300    7499   20-FEB-81
JONES    MANAGER    2975          7566   02-APR-81
MARTIN   SALESMAN   1250  1400    7654   28-SEP-81
SMITH    CLERK       800          7369   17-DEC-80
WARD     SALESMAN   1250   500    7521   22-FEB-81
```

Write your answer here:

Exercise 5.3

This request is more difficult. Show the employee information (EMPNO, ENAME, JOB, SAL) and the salary grade for all employees. (Hint: Which table contains salary grade? How can you join to that table?)

RESULT TABLE:

EMPNO	ENAME	JOB	SAL	GRADE
7369	SMITH	CLERK	800	1
7876	ADAMS	CLERK	1100	1
7900	JAMES	CLERK	950	1
7521	WARD	SALESMAN	1250	2
7654	MARTIN	SALESMAN	1250	2
7934	MILLER	CLERK	1300	2
7499	ALLEN	SALESMAN	1600	3
7844	TURNER	SALESMAN	1500	3
7566	JONES	MANAGER	2975	4
7698	BLAKE	MANAGER	2850	4
7782	CLARK	MANAGER	2450	4
7788	SCOTT	ANALYST	3000	4
7902	FORD	ANALYST	3000	4
7839	KING	PRESIDENT	5000	5

Write your answer here:

____

____

____

____

____

____

Exercise 5.4

We mentioned a cartesian product in the Exercise 5.3 notes section. In this exercise, we'll examine cartesians further. First, we will look at a complete cartesian product of two full tables. Join together the DEPT and SALGRADE tables with no join variable. Show all columns and sort by GRADE and LOC.

RESULT TABLE:

DEPTNO	DNAME	LOC	GRADE	LOSAL	HISAL
40	OPERATIONS	BOSTON	1	700	1200
30	SALES	CHICAGO	1	700	1200
20	RESEARCH	DALLAS	1	700	1200
10	ACCOUNTING	NEW YORK	1	700	1200
40	OPERATIONS	BOSTON	2	1201	1400
30	SALES	CHICAGO	2	1201	1400
20	RESEARCH	DALLAS	2	1201	1400
10	ACCOUNTING	NEW YORK	2	1201	1400
40	OPERATIONS	BOSTON	3	1401	2000
30	SALES	CHICAGO	3	1401	2000
20	RESEARCH	DALLAS	3	1401	2000
10	ACCOUNTING	NEW YORK	3	1401	2000
40	OPERATIONS	BOSTON	4	2001	3000
30	SALES	CHICAGO	4	2001	3000
20	RESEARCH	DALLAS	4	2001	3000
10	ACCOUNTING	NEW YORK	4	2001	3000
40	OPERATIONS	BOSTON	5	3001	9999
30	SALES	CHICAGO	5	3001	9999
20	RESEARCH	DALLAS	5	3001	9999
10	ACCOUNTING	NEW YORK	5	3001	9999

Write your answer here:

Exercise 5.5

A cartesian can be partial and still have limited value. Show the department information alongside the EMPNO, ENAME, and JOB columns from the EMP table, but only for employees with an "R" in their name and only departments with a "C" in the name. Don't include a join predicate. (Hint: Use LIKE predicates.)

RESULT TABLE:

EMPNO	ENAME	JOB	DEPTNO	DNAME	LOC
7521	WARD	SALESMAN	10	ACCOUNTING	NEW YORK
7654	MARTIN	SALESMAN	10	ACCOUNTING	NEW YORK
7782	CLARK	MANAGER	10	ACCOUNTING	NEW YORK
7844	TURNER	SALESMAN	10	ACCOUNTING	NEW YORK
7902	FORD	ANALYST	10	ACCOUNTING	NEW YORK
7934	MILLER	CLERK	10	ACCOUNTING	NEW YORK
7521	WARD	SALESMAN	20	RESEARCH	DALLAS
7654	MARTIN	SALESMAN	20	RESEARCH	DALLAS
7782	CLARK	MANAGER	20	RESEARCH	DALLAS
7844	TURNER	SALESMAN	20	RESEARCH	DALLAS
7902	FORD	ANALYST	20	RESEARCH	DALLAS
7934	MILLER	CLERK	20	RESEARCH	DALLAS

Write your answer here:

____

____

____

____

____

____

Exercise 5.6

There is a category of problems that requires a join that is not an equal join (sometimes called an "equijoin"). It uses a cartesian with an inequality predicate such as " > ", or a parent-to-child link. Solve this request: "I'm putting together the annual senior staff golf tournament. List all possible pairs of staff earning over $2000 in salary, so that it shows a staffer on the left with one on the right who earns less."

Show ENAME and SALARY for both in the pair. Label the columns "HI_NAME," "HI_SAL," "LO_NAME," and "LO_SAL." Sort the report so that the HI_SAL column goes from highest to lowest. (Hint: Join the table to itself.)

RESULT TABLE:

```
HI_NAME      HI_SAL     LO_NAME     LO_SAL
--------     ------     -------     ------
KING           5000     JONES         2975
KING           5000     BLAKE         2850
KING           5000     CLARK         2450
KING           5000     FORD          3000
KING           5000     SCOTT         3000
SCOTT          3000     JONES         2975
FORD           3000     BLAKE         2850
SCOTT          3000     BLAKE         2850
FORD           3000     CLARK         2450
SCOTT          3000     CLARK         2450
FORD           3000     JONES         2975
JONES          2975     BLAKE         2850
JONES          2975     CLARK         2450
BLAKE          2850     CLARK         2450
```

Write your answer here:

Exercise 5.7

To improve performance you may want to convert a subquery into a join. "Sum the SAL of all employees working for departments in CHICAGO" yields the subquery:

```
SELECT SUM(SAL) "CHI SAL" FROM EMP
WHERE DEPTNO IN
  (SELECT DEPTNO FROM DEPT WHERE LOC = 'CHICAGO');
```

Make this subquery into a join.

RESULT TABLE:

```
CHI SAL
-------
   9400
```

Write your answer here:

___

___

___

___

___

___

Exercise 5.8

Recall in our previous lesson we showed the following correlated subquery:

```
SELECT DEPTNO, DNAME, LOC FROM DEPT D WHERE EXISTS
  (SELECT M.* FROM EMP M, EMP E
  WHERE M.EMPNO = E.MGR
  AND M.DEPTNO = D.DEPTNO
  AND M.HIREDATE > E.HIREDATE);
```

Now show the departments (DEPTNO, DNAME, and LOC) that have a manager (or managers) hired after one of the manager's subordinates. Rewrite this solution as a join.

RESULT TABLE:

DEPTNO	DNAME	LOC
10	ACCOUNTING	NEW YORK
20	RESEARCH	DALLAS
30	SALES	CHICAGO

Write your answer here:

____

____

____

____

____

____

Exercise 5.9

This is another correlated subquery from a previous lesson that you should be able to convert to a join.

```
SELECT DEPTNO, DNAME, LOC FROM DEPT D
WHERE 4 <=
  (SELECT COUNT(*)
  FROM EMP E WHERE E.DEPTNO = D.DEPTNO);
```

Show the departments (DEPTNO, DNAME, and LOC) that have at least four employees assigned. (Hint: Move the COUNT(*) to a HAVING clause.)

RESULT TABLE:

```
DEPTNO   DNAME      LOC
------   --------   -------
    20   RESEARCH   DALLAS
    30   SALES      CHICAGO
```

Write your answer here:

Exercise 5.10

While we are practicing GROUP BY, recall that you can aggregate results using data from two tables that you join together. Now show each department name, the number of employees in it, and the total department salary, along with the minimum and maximum salary in the department. Name the columns "DEPT," "HEADCNT," "TOT SAL," "MIN SAL," and "MAX SAL."

RESULT TABLE:

```
DEPT          HEADCNT    TOT SAL    MIN SAL    MAX SAL
----------    -------    -------    -------    -------
ACCOUNTING          3       8750       1300       5000
RESEARCH            5      10875        800       3000
SALES               6       9400        950       2850
```

Write your answer here:

____

____

____

____

____

____

Congratulations! You've completed the chapter on the advanced use of joins. To practice these concepts in a simulated SQL environment, choose Menu Item 1 from Exercise Disk 2.

Solutions to Workshop Exercises

Exercise 5.1 - Solution

```
SELECT E.DEPTNO, D.DNAME, D.LOC,
E.EMPNO, E.ENAME, E.JOB
FROM EMP E, DEPT D
WHERE E.DEPTNO = D.DEPTNO
ORDER BY E.DEPTNO;
```

Notes

The three basic rules for a join follow, including examples from our answer above:

1. Name the two (or more) tables or views in the FROM clause, separated by commas. A table label or alias may be specified after each table name.

Example:

```
FROM EMP E, DEPT D
```

Tables EMP and DEPT are specified for the join. The sequence in which they are written does not matter. Aliases are assigned as E and D respectively.

2. Specify one join variable with its predicate for each column participating in the join. Usually the predicate is an equal comparison.

Example:

```
WHERE E.DEPTNO = D.DEPTNO
```

We request that rows from E be joined to rows of D whenever the values in the DEPTNO columns of both rows are equal. The sequence of E and D is not important.

3. We fully qualify any references to a column with its table name or alias if the column name is ambiguous; that is, if the name appears in two or more tables that the query references.

Example:

```
SELECT E.DEPTNO, D.DNAME, D.LOC, ...
       WHERE E.DEPTNO = D.DEPTNO
       ORDER BY E.DEPTNO
```

We needed to qualify only one column (DEPTNO) because that was the only name appearing in both the EMP and DEPT tables. Any other column names that we qualified in our answer were qualified simply to improve the documentation of what we were doing; that is, to document from which table the column came.

Exercise 5.2 - Solution

```
SELECT B.ENAME, B.JOB, B.SAL, B.COMM,
E.EMPNO, E.HIREDATE
FROM EMP E, BONUS B
WHERE E.ENAME = B.ENAME
AND E.JOB = B.JOB;
```

Notes

The design of this BONUS table is poor. A last name is not a good primary key, because it will not necessarily uniquely identify each row of most tables containing names. The EMP table has the EMPNO column as a unique key column, so EMPNO should have been included in our BONUS table.

In our small sample tables, all the names are unique, but joining on name alone is a technique that usually won't work, because many last names appear more than once. So we've used both the EMPNO and the JOB columns together to perform the join:

```
WHERE E.ENAME = B.ENAME
AND E.JOB = B.JOB
```

Because there were two columns being joined, two join variables were used, each with an equal comparison.

Exercise 5.3 - Solution

```
SELECT E.EMPNO, E.ENAME, E.JOB, E.SAL, G.GRADE
FROM EMP E, SALGRADE G
WHERE E.SAL BETWEEN G.LOSAL AND G.HISAL;
```

Notes

This answer uses the BETWEEN predicate to perform the join. In practice, the BETWEEN predicate may not perform efficiently with large tables in some SQL systems. (We've shown a second solution below.) In the answer above, the program joins each E.SAL value to its appropriate SALGRADE row by finding the row in which the E.SAL falls between the two salary range values, LOSAL and HISAL.

A solution without BETWEEN is:

```
SELECT E.EMPNO, E.ENAME, E.JOB, E.SAL, G.GRADE
FROM EMP E, SALGRADE G
WHERE E.SAL >= G.LOSAL
AND E.SAL <= G.HISAL;
```

This query may work faster if the SQL system uses an index on the G.LOSAL columns (assuming indexes are defined).

In this solution the basic join starts with an inequality comparison " >= " which, by itself, would produce a cartesian product. The system would combine the E row with every G row with a LOSAL greater than or equal to the E.SAL value.

The last predicate, the " <= " inequality, limits the cartesian product to just one row, just like an equal join.

Exercise 5.4 - Solution

```
SELECT D.*, G.*
FROM DEPT D, SALGRADE G
ORDER BY G.GRADE, D.LOC;
```

Notes

As you can see from the results, the cartesian product takes one row from the first table (or subset of table rows) and combines it with every row of the second table (or subset of table rows). This would be very inefficient if the tables were large. The results produce a results table equal to the product of the number of rows in one set times the number of rows in the other set.

Notice the SELECT clause:

```
SELECT D.*, G.*
```

It uses a special form of the " * " notation. Usually SELECT * means "produce a results table having every column from my table in the order in which the columns were created." With two tables, the format D.*, G.* tells the system to first present all of the columns from the D table and then all of the columns from the G table.

Exercise 5.5 - Solution

```
SELECT E.EMPNO, E.ENAME, E.JOB, D.*
FROM EMP E, DEPT D
WHERE E.ENAME LIKE '%R%'
AND D.DNAME LIKE '%C%';
```

Notes

The results show 12 rows. The EMP table had a subset of six rows for WARD, MARTIN, CLARK, TURNER, FORD, and MILLER, all of whom have an "R" in their name. The "C" subset from DEPT was formed with the two departments ACCOUNTING and RESEARCH. The cartesian combines the six employees with the two departments in all 12 combinations.

Exercise 5.6 - Solution

```
SELECT H.ENAME "HI_NAME", H.SAL "HI_SAL",
L.ENAME "LO_NAME", L.SAL "LO_SAL"
FROM EMP H, EMP L
WHERE L.SAL > 2000
AND H.SAL > 2000
AND H.SAL > L.SAL
ORDER BY H.SAL DESC;
```

Notes

In this exercise we are dealing with a subset joined to itself. We've given both versions of the EMP table aliases: H for the high-salary employee and L for the low-salary employee.

The inequality predicate:

```
AND H.SAL > L.SAL
```

ensures that we won't get two pairs that are mirror images of each other (e.g., CLARK & BLAKE, or BLAKE & CLARK), or an identical pair (e.g., CLARK & CLARK or BLAKE & BLAKE). Either BLAKE's salary is greater than CLARK's or CLARK's is greater than BLAKE's.

What if BLAKE's salary equals CLARK's? They won't be paired together for this query.

Without the inequality predicate, we would have a partial cartesian similar to the previous exercise.

Exercise 5.7 - Solution

```
SELECT SUM(E.SAL) "CHI SAL"
FROM EMP E, DEPT D
WHERE E.DEPTNO = D.DEPTNO
AND D.LOC = 'CHICAGO';
```

Notes

Once you've joined two tables together, you may think of the input to your WHERE clause as a wide row of data from the first table followed by data from the second table:

```
<——row from EMP——><——row from DEPT——>
```

In this format, LOC is easily compared directly.

So why do a join instead of the subquery? There are two basic reasons, the relevance of which will depend upon the SQL system implementation you are using.

1. Certain predicates do not use indexes if a subquery is involved. For large tables this could hamper performance.
2. A join tends to use indexes more than a subquery. A join will generally run faster for large tables than a subquery, when there is a WHERE clause to filter out rows to be joined, and when indexes help the filtering and the joining processes.

Exercise 5.8 - Solution

```
SELECT DISTINCT D.DEPTNO, D.DNAME, D.LOC
FROM DEPT D, EMP M, EMP E
WHERE M.EMPNO = E.MGR
AND M.DEPTNO = D.DEPTNO
AND M.HIREDATE > E.HIREDATE;
```

Notes

There is an advantage to using the join solution rather than the subquery (repeated below).

Subquery:

```
SELECT DEPTNO, DNAME, LOC FROM DEPT D WHERE EXISTS
  (SELECT M.* FROM EMP M, EMP E
  WHERE M.EMPNO = E.MGR
  AND M.DEPTNO = D.DEPTNO
  AND M.HIREDATE > E.HIREDATE);
```

When a query uses a subquery based on another table or tables, it can only present results from the outer query table (or tables, if the outer query is a join). With the join solution we can easily add to our results the names of the managers hired after subordinates and even the name of the subordinate hired earlier.

Join:

```
SELECT DISTINCT D.DEPTNO, D.DNAME, D.LOC,
M.ENAME, M.HIREDATE,
E.ENAME, E.HIREDATE
FROM DEPT D, EMP M, EMP E ...
```

Why did we use DISTINCT in our SELECT clause in the main answer? The subquery solution presents a single row of the outer table when the subquery finds a TRUE (meaning there was at least one row in the subquery that existed).

The join solution will return each of the matching rows in tables E and M joined with the results row from D. If there were two or more managers found in one department that met our criteria, then the department row in the results would appear two or more times unless you use DISTINCT. By using DISTINCT, we remove duplicate rows from the results.

Exercise 5.9 - Solution

```
SELECT D.DEPTNO, D.DNAME, D.LOC
FROM DEPT D, EMP E
WHERE E.DEPTNO = D.DEPTNO
GROUP BY D.DEPTNO, D.DNAME, D.LOC
HAVING COUNT(*) >= 4;
```

Notes

Do you remember why all three columns, DEPTNO, DNAME, and LOC, appear in the GROUP BY clause? Because we want them to appear in the SELECT clause, SQL requires that the columns named in the SELECT clause (which are not in functions) must be named in the GROUP BY clause.

In the DEPT table the three column values DEPTNO, DNAME, and LOC change together from row to row. Thus, grouping by all three column values gives the same result as grouping by DEPTNO alone.

Exercise 5.10 - Solution

```
SELECT D.DNAME DEPT, COUNT(*) HEADCNT,
SUM(E.SAL) "TOT SAL",
MIN(E.SAL) "MIN SAL",
MAX(E.SAL) "MAX SAL"
FROM DEPT D, EMP E
WHERE D.DEPTNO = E.DEPTNO
GROUP BY D.DNAME;
```

Notes

When performing this kind of query, it is important to remember that the SQL system treats a join as if the rows of the two or more tables were joined together in one seamless new row:

```
<——row from DEPT——><——row from EMP——>
```

The data in the new row may be operated on by most of the SQL features. In this case we are using GROUP BY function. The results contain column functions about data from the EMP table while displaying descriptive information from the DEPT table, the department name.

At this point it is relevant to discuss the subject of views. In most of the exercises above, one or both of the tables being joined could have been replaced by a view if a few rules were followed. A view may be a column and row subset. Such a view shows all (or just some) columns and all (or just some) rows from one table:

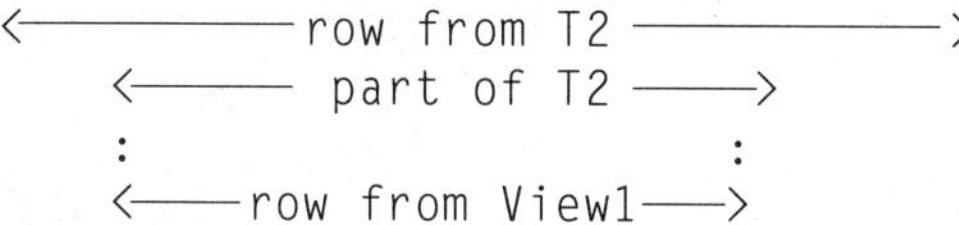

There is never a problem substituting such a view for a table in a join:

```
                  <——————— row from T2 ———————>
                          <——— part of T2 ———>
                          :                  :
<——row from T1 ——><——row from View1 ——>
```

A view that is a join of two (or more) such partial tables should itself result in a column and row subset join view:

```
<——row from T2 ——><———row from T3 ———>
  <—part of T2 ——><—part of T3->
  :                          :
  <——————— row from View2————>
```

It, too, will pose no problem being used in place of one table in a join:

```
                  <——row from T2 ——><——— row from T3——>
                    <—part of T2——><—part of T3->
                    :                             :
<——row from T1——><—————— row from View2 ————>
```

The join then becomes a join of three tables.

A warning is necessary. If the view were built using the GROUP BY feature, be aware that most systems don't allow the substitution of the view for a table in a join. Why not? Because the view's definition is combined with the join specification and the result would be invalid SQL syntax. Be careful!

6

Introduction to Transaction Controls

In this chapter you will be introduced to the management of transactions. Transaction control is the issuing of commands to reverse database changes. The commands discussed in this chapter are COMMIT, AUTOCOMMIT, and ROLLBACK.

TRANSACTIONS

This chapter concerns the management of transactions in an ORACLE RDBMS. The AUTOCOMMIT feature is unique to the ORACLE RDBMS, but COMMIT and ROLLBACK are statements that you will find in all relational database management systems.

A transaction is a change to the database such as an INSERT, UPDATE, or DELETE operation. A transaction can be a single operation, or it may consist of a series of operations that change the database.

For example, suppose you execute the following SQL statements:

```
UPDATE EMP
SET SAL = SAL * 1.10;

DELETE FROM BONUS
WHERE ENAME = 'CLARK';
```

Together, the UPDATE and DELETE operations constitute a transaction (a change to the database). Either operation by itself is a transaction, if it is executed separately.

Transactions are normally made permanent when you exit ORACLE's SQL*Plus. They are also made permanent when you execute one of the following commands:

```
ALTER, AUDIT, CREATE, DISCONNECT, DROP, EXIT, GRANT,
NOAUDIT, QUIT, or REVOKE
```

Transaction control is the issuing of commands that make a permanent database change, and that reverse database changes.

You can make database changes permanent at any time by using the COMMIT statement.

You can have changes to the database committed (made permanent) automatically with the AUTOCOMMIT feature of ORACLE.

You can roll back (reverse) any changes that have not been committed with the ROLLBACK command.

Prior to committing changes, it may appear that changes you have made to the database are permanent because you can see the results in your tables.

However, if another user queries one of your tables prior to your making the changes permanent, that user will not see the changes.

Furthermore, you can roll back these transactions if you change your mind or make a mistake.

COMMIT

First, let's look at how to make database changes permanent.

Here is the syntax for the COMMIT command:

```
COMMIT;
```

You will see the message "commit complete" once this command is executed.

Any changes made before the issuing of a COMMIT become permanent once the COMMIT is executed.

In the example at the beginning of this lesson, an UPDATE and then a DELETE operation are carried out. If you wanted the UPDATE to be made permanent, type COMMIT immediately after the UPDATE:

```
    UPDATE EMP
    SET SAL = SAL * 1.10
    COMMIT;
commit complete

    DELETE FROM BONUS
    WHERE ENAME = 'CLARK';
```

The result of the UPDATE has been made permanent. The result of the DELETE operation has not been made permanent, because a COMMIT has not been issued.

The UPDATE cannot be reversed, because it has been committed, but the DELETE can be reversed because it has not been committed.

AUTOCOMMIT

ORACLE gives you the option of automatically committing transactions. You can do this with the **AUTOCOMMIT** feature. If AUTOCOMMIT is on, each change made by an INSERT, UPDATE, or DELETE operation is immediately committed.

Here is the syntax for AUTOCOMMIT:

```
SET AUTOCOMMIT IMMEDIATE;  Activates AUTOCOMMIT
SET AUTOCOMMIT ON;         Activates AUTOCOMMIT
SET AUTOCOMMIT OFF;        Deactivates AUTOCOMMIT
```

If you want to check the status of AUTOCOMMIT, type:

```
SHOW AUTOCOMMIT;
```

You will see either "autocommit IMMEDIATE" or "autocommit OFF", depending on AUTOCOMMIT's status.

Here is an example of the use of the AUTOCOMMIT feature.

If you want all subsequent INSERTs, UPDATEs, and DELETEs to be automatically committed, enter either SET AUTOCOMMIT IMMEDIATE; or SET AUTOCOMMIT ON;

```
SET AUTOCOMMIT ON;
```

Next enter a DELETE statement to remove information about WARD from the EMP table:

```
DELETE FROM EMP
WHERE ENAME = 'WARD';
```

The DELETE operation is automatically committed. There is no way to reverse it.

To return information about WARD to the EMP table, you have to use the INSERT statement.

If you no longer want changes to the database to be automatically committed, type the following:

```
SET AUTOCOMMIT OFF;
```

When AUTOCOMMIT is off, subsequent changes to the database are not permanent until a COMMIT is issued or the user exits the database.

ROLLBACK

Now, let's look at the command that allows you to reverse changes to the database, when these transactions have not yet been committed. This command is **ROLLBACK**. Here is the syntax for this command:

```
ROLLBACK;
```

The message "rollback complete" appears after this command is executed.

Suppose you want to delete one row of the EMP table. By mistake, you enter the following:

```
DELETE FROM EMP;
```

Unfortunately, this deletes the entire contents of the EMP table.

If you now type:

```
ROLLBACK;
```

and AUTOCOMMIT is off, the change made by the DELETE statement is reversed. The EMP table is then restored to the state it was in before the DELETE was executed, and you have another opportunity to delete the specific row you intended to delete. If AUTOCOMMIT was on during this, the changes would have been committed and you would not have been able to roll back the changes.

INTERACTION OF COMMIT, AUTOCOMMIT, ROLLBACK

How often should you commit changes to the database?

When you are working on a specific task, and then plan to start an unrelated task, it is a good idea to commit all changes after the first task is completed. This prevents you from losing the work completed during the first task, if power is lost or if you make a mistake during the second task and are forced to use ROLLBACK.

When you are working on one very large task, commit your changes periodically to avoid losing work in the event power is lost or a mistake is made and changes must be rolled back.

These two strategies are good rules of computing in SQL.

Next, let's look at how COMMIT, AUTOCOMMIT, and ROLLBACK interact.

This first example demonstrates how the result of an insert can be reversed.

Suppose that AUTOCOMMIT is off. You can verify that AUTOCOMMIT is off by typing:

```
SHOW AUTOCOMMIT;
```

The message "autocommit OFF" appears.

Suppose you want to add another category to the SALGRADE table to reflect increasing salaries at your company. This new grade is designated as grade 6, with a low salary of $10,000 and a high salary of $11,000. Here is the SQL statement that adds this category to SALGRADE:

```
INSERT INTO SALGRADE (GRADE, LOSAL, HISAL)
VALUES (6, 10000, 11000);
```

If you enter

```
SELECT * FROM SALGRADE;
```

you see the following:

```
    GRADE     LOSAL     HISAL
  -------   -------   -------
        1       700      1200
        2      1201      1400
        3      1401      2000
        4      2001      3000
        5      3001      9999
        6     10000     11000
```

But, after you take another look at the memo from personnel regarding the new salary grade, you see that the new salary range should be from $10,000 to $12,000, not $10,000 to $11,000.

Should you delete the row just inserted into the SALGRADE table?

That's one solution to your problem, but here is another approach.

Remember that AUTOCOMMIT is set to OFF. Therefore, although your change is reflected in the SALGRADE table, the change is not permanent.

To reverse your change, type the following:

```
ROLLBACK;
```

The message "rollback complete" appears.

Now, again enter

```
SELECT * FROM SALGRADE;
```

to see the original table.

GRADE	LOSAL	HISAL
1	700	1200
2	1201	1400
3	1401	2000
4	2001	3000
5	3001	9999

The additional row in SALGRADE has not been made a permanent part of the table, even though you saw it when you queried SALGRADE.

Now enter the correct INSERT statement for the new salary grade.

Here's what happens if AUTOCOMMIT is on. Remember, you activate AUTOCOMMIT by typing the following:

```
SET AUTOCOMMIT ON;
```

If you type

```
    SHOW AUTOCOMMIT;
autocommit IMMEDIATE
```

the message "autocommit IMMEDIATE" appears. This message means that AUTOCOMMIT is on.

Next, suppose employee Ward has been paid her bonus, and, therefore should be removed from the BONUS table. Enter the following to remove Ward's record from BONUS:

```
DELETE FROM BONUS
WHERE ENAME = 'WARD';
```

To see the contents of BONUS, type:

```
SELECT * FROM BONUS;
```

and the following appears:

ENAME	JOB	SAL	COMM
SMITH	CLERK	800	
ALLEN	SALESMAN	1600	300
JONES	MANAGER	2975	
MARTIN	SALESMAN	1250	1400

Ward's record is gone. If you have made a mistake and Ward was not the employee to receive the bonus, you cannot roll back the transaction. If you issue a ROLLBACK command, you see the "rollback complete" message, but Ward's record is permanently deleted from BONUS.

Because AUTOCOMMIT is on, the DELETE is automatically committed. Your only recourse in the event of a mistake is to INSERT the data again.

Now, let's suppose that AUTOCOMMIT is off.

If you type

```
SHOW AUTOCOMMIT;
```

the "autocommit OFF" message appears.

The following example demonstrates that ROLLBACK reverses changes made since the last COMMIT was executed.

The sales department of your company is moving from Chicago to Indianapolis. This department is also changing its name from "Sales" to "Sales and Marketing."

To change the LOC value for the sales department in the DEPT table, enter the following update statement:

```
UPDATE DEPT
SET LOC = 'INDIANAPOLIS'
WHERE DEPTNO = 30;
```

You can see the result of this update when you enter

```
SELECT * FROM DEPT
```

```
 DEPTNO  DNAME           LOC
-------  --------------  -------------
     10  ACCOUNTING      NEW YORK
     20  RESEARCH        DALLAS
     30  SALES           INDIANAPOLIS
     40  OPERATIONS      BOSTON
```

Check to see that Indianapolis is spelled correctly, and you commit this change:

```
COMMIT;
```

A "commit complete" message indicates that the commit is successful.

Next, make the second change. Change the name of the sales department to "Sales and Marketing." Use the code SALES/MKTNG in the DEPT table.

```
UPDATE DEPT
SET DNAME = 'SALES/MKTNG'
WHERE DEPTNO = 30;
```

Check the result of this update by entering the following:

```
SELECT * FROM DEPT;
```

```
DEPTNO  DNAME            LOC
------- ---------------- -------------
     10 ACCOUNTING       NEW YORK
     20 RESEARCH         DALLAS
     30 SALES/MKTNG      INDIANAPOLIS
     40 OPERATIONS       BOSTON
```

Because you have not committed this second operation yet, you can roll back this change. ROLLBACK this transaction by entering:

```
ROLLBACK;
```

The "rollback complete" message appears. Now, when you enter

```
SELECT * FROM DEPT;
```

you see:

```
DEPTNO  DNAME            LOC
------- ---------------- -------------
     10 ACCOUNTING       NEW YORK
     20 RESEARCH         DALLAS
     30 SALES            INDIANAPOLIS
     40 OPERATIONS       BOSTON
```

Notice that the result of the first update operation, where CHICAGO was changed to INDIANAPOLIS, is still in the DEPT table. That is because the first change was committed, or made permanent.

The second change, from SALES to SALES/MKTNG, was not committed. Therefore, the second change was rolled back. Even though the change was reflected when you first queried the DEPT table, you have not made it permanent.

In this chapter, you learned how to:

- Identify transactions as changes to the database
- Use the COMMIT command to make changes permanent
- Employ the AUTOCOMMIT feature
- Explain the interaction of COMMIT, AUTOCOMMIT, ROLLBACK

Now let's practice these concepts with some workshop exercises.

Workshop Exercises

Introduction to Transaction Controls

In this section, you will practice the following concepts:

1. The use of ORACLE's AUTOCOMMIT feature
2. The use of ROLLBACK
3. The use of COMMIT

All changes to the database between successive COMMIT and/or ROLLBACK operations are called a transaction. For example, suppose you start your RDBMS, make several updates, commit them, add several new rows, and exit. The updates constitute one transaction, the insertions another.

When a transaction is interrupted by a serious error, the entire transaction is automatically rolled back. This prevents the error from causing unwanted changes to your data, and returns your tables to their status at the time of the last COMMIT. By doing this, your RDBMS protects the integrity of your tables.

This section concerns the use of the commands that accomplish transaction control: COMMIT, ROLLBACK, and AUTOCOMMIT.

Exercise 6.1

We can control how changes to the database are made permanent with the SET AUTOCOMMIT command. Find out what the AUTOCOMMIT status is now. (Hint: Use the SHOW command.)

RESULT:

```
autocommit OFF
```

Write your answer here:

Exercise 6.2

Assume AUTOCOMMIT is ON. We'll create a new test table for these next few exercises.

Name the new table TESTA and have only one column, AA, which holds a NUMBER. Show the empty table.

RESULT:

```
no records selected
```

Write your answer here:

____

____

____

____

____

____

Exercise 6.3

With AUTOCOMMIT set to ON, we should be able to insert new rows into the TESTA table. Use the SQL INSERT statement to add rows with the values found in DEPTNO in table DEPT. Show the contents of TESTA. (Hint: Use a single INSERT statement with a SELECT built in, instead of four INSERTS, each with VALUES clauses.)

RESULT:

```
4 records created.

      AA
--------
      10
      20
      30
      40
```

Write your answer here:

____

____

____

____

____

____

Exercise 6.4

Now, with AUTOCOMMIT ON and the previous exercise complete, issue an SQL ROLLBACK statement and list the contents of TESTA.

RESULT TABLE:

```
rollback complete

      AA
--------
      10
      20
      30
      40
```

Write your answer here:

___

___

___

___

___

___

Exercise 6.5

SET AUTOCOMMIT OFF and insert a new row with the value 100 and COMMIT the revision. INSERT a second new row for 200, but don't COMMIT that row. List the TESTA table.

RESULT:

```
1 record created.
commit complete
1 record created.

      AA
--------
      10
      20
      30
      40
     100
     200
```

Write your answer here:

____

____

____

____

____

____

Exercise 6.6

With AUTOCOMMIT OFF issue a ROLLBACK statement and list the TESTA table.

RESULT:

```
rollback complete

      AA
--------
      10
      20
      30
      40
     100
          ← row 200 is gone
```

Write your answer here:

____

____

____

____

____

____

Exercise 6.7

With AUTOCOMMIT OFF, issue a DELETE from TESTA for the row in which AA has the value 100. Don't commit the change. List the table.

RESULT:

```
1 record deleted.

      AA
--------
      10
      20
      30
      40
```

Write your answer here:

____

____

____

____

____

____

Exercise 6.8

With AUTOCOMMIT OFF, issue a ROLLBACK statement and list the TESTA table.

RESULT:

```
rollback complete

      AA
--------
      10
      20
      30
      40
     100 (row 100 is back)
```

Write your answer here:

Exercise 6.9

With AUTOCOMMIT OFF, issue a DROP TABLE statement and remove the TESTA table from the database.

RESULT:

```
Table dropped.
```

Write your answer here:

Congratulations! You have completed this chapter on transaction controls. To practice transaction controls in a simulated SQL environment, choose Menu Item 2 from Exercise Disk 2.

Solutions to Workshop Exercises

Exercise 6.1 - Solution

```
SHOW AUTOCOMMIT;
```

Notes

ORACLE's SQL*Plus allows you to control many features dynamically. Each feature is controlled by setting a system variable, such as AUTOCOMMIT.

You can display the current status of any system variable by issuing the SHOW command.

AUTOCOMMIT tells the system to ensure that all changes to the database are made permanent after each SQL statement. AUTOCOMMIT can be SET to either:

OFF (or ALL)	The system expects you to do any COMMITs that are needed.
ON (or IMMEDIATE)	The system does a COMMIT after each SQL statement.

Exercise 6.2 - Solution

```
CREATE TABLE TESTA (AA NUMBER);
SELECT * FROM TESTA;
```

Notes

Some SQL systems show an empty results table like this:

```
        AA
----------
```

If you want to see what columns are in TESTA, issue the SQL*Plus DESCRIBE command

```
DESCRIBE TESTA;
```

It shows you the name of each column, whether or not it is NULL, and the datatype assigned to the column, such as:

```
Name                             Null ?   Type
-------------------------------- -------- ----
AA                                        Number
```

When the CREATE TABLE SQL statement is executed, the ORACLE system updates many system tables, collectively known as its catalog. The SQL*Plus DESCRIBE command reads rows from those catalog tables and displays information for you.

CREATE and DROP statements ignore the setting of AUTOCOMMIT and force a COMMIT for those statements, as well as any other prior statements not yet committed.

Exercise 6.3 - Solution

```
SET AUTOCOMMIT ON;
INSERT INTO TESTA (AA)
  SELECT DEPTNO FROM DEPT;
SELECT * FROM TESTA;
```

Notes

The INSERT statement has a SELECT clause with a single results column, DEPTNO, which loads into the single target column, AA.

We could have entered four INSERT statements such as:

```
INSERT INTO TESTA (AA) VALUES (10);
INSERT INTO TESTA (AA) VALUES (20);
INSERT INTO TESTA (AA) VALUES (30);
INSERT INTO TESTA (AA) VALUES (40);
```

AUTOCOMMIT would force each of these inserts into the database as soon as the query was completed.

Exercise 6.4 - Solution

```
ROLLBACK;
SELECT * FROM TESTA;
```

Notes

The ROLLBACK did not reverse the action of the INSERT statement (or four INSERT statements), because the new rows were automatically committed after the INSERT operation. There were no new rows still uncommitted to be rolled back. We see all the four rows still in the table.

Exercise 6.5 - Solution

```
SET AUTOCOMMIT OFF;
INSERT INTO TESTA (AA) VALUES (100);
COMMIT;
INSERT INTO TESTA (AA) VALUES (200);
SELECT * FROM TESTA;
```

Notes

COMMIT and ROLLBACK are part of the transaction control mechanism provided by an RDBMS. Each transaction is a group of records that must be entered into the database together as a group or not entered at all.

The rows 100 and 200 might be line items from an invoice that should update the database together or not at all. We see our new rows in the table, but remember that the last row with 200 is not yet committed. If the power failed at this moment, the system would recover the rows up to the 100, but the 200 would not be recovered into the database.

Recovery is one reason for having transaction controls. We want recovery to work on completed transactions; that is, transactions that have been intentionally COMMITed to the database. A partial transaction should never be committed or it may leave the database "broken" if the recovery mechanism is attempted.

Exercise 6.6 - Solution

```
SET AUTOCOMMIT OFF;
ROLLBACK;
SELECT * FROM TESTA;
```

Notes

The last row, 200, which was uncommitted, has been backed out of the database. We are now at a point of consistency, a point at which everything in our table is committed.

Exercise 6.7 - Solution

```
SET AUTOCOMMIT OFF;
DELETE FROM TESTA WHERE AA = 100;
SELECT * FROM TESTA;
```

Notes

As expected, 100, which was previously committed, is no longer shown in our table.

But remember that just as 200 was an uncommitted insertion in our prior exercise, now 100 is an uncommitted deletion.

Note that there was no need to issue another SET AUTO OFF command. The AUTOCOMMIT system variable remains set until you either change it or log off of SQL*Plus.

Exercise 6.8 - Solution

```
SET AUTOCOMMIT OFF;
ROLLBACK;
SELECT * FROM TESTA;
```

Notes

For this exercise, row 100 is back in the table, even though we had DELETED row 100 in the previous exercise.

Row 100 was never deleted completely until that transaction (which contained the DELETE statement) was committed to the database. But before the transaction was finalized with a COMMIT, we chose to reverse our action by issuing a ROLLBACK. This is the second reason for transaction controls, to allow for a "change of heart" in the midst of a transaction.

For example, we could push the CANCEL key on a teller machine before the money was issued. Or we could enter an order and have to cancel it when its total amount exceeded a credit limit for the account. Most real-life systems need to have that "cancel" option, which means the transaction must be rolled back to its start point.

Each ROLLBACK leaves the database at a point of consistency at which no uncommitted changes have been partially entered.

Exercise 6.9 - Solution

```
SET AUTOCOMMIT OFF;
DROP TABLE TESTA;
```

Notes

We have gone full circle. We created a table, loaded some data rows, changed those rows, and then dropped the table. Along the way we learned how to use the COMMIT and ROLLBACK statements from standard SQL, and the SET AUTOCOMMIT command from SQL*Plus.

7

Tables

This chapter begins with a review of tables, covering valid table names and the CREATE TABLE statement. After the review, ORACLE features such as CREATE TABLE AS SELECT and DESCRIBE are examined. Finally, the COMMENT ON and ALTER TABLE commands are discussed.

REVIEW OF DEFINING TABLES

Remember that information in a relational database is stored in tables, and a table is a data structure consisting of rows and columns.

Each column contains one kind of information. For example, the EMPNO column in the EMP table contains employee numbers.

Each row contains one set of information. The information is stored in individual fields, each represented by a column of the table. For example, the EMPNO field in a row represents the EMPNO column.

Let's look at how tables are created in a relational database. Here is the standard syntax for the CREATE TABLE command, from the SQL Data Definition Language:

```
CREATE TABLE <table_name>
(<column_name_1> <datatype> [NOT NULL],
<column_name_2> <datatype> [NOT NULL],
...          ...
<column_name_n> <datatype> [NOT NULL]);
```

The keywords CREATE TABLE are followed by the name of the table to be created.

There are several rules to be considered when naming a table. (These rules are the same as those for naming an ORACLE database object.) A table name:

- Must begin with a letter, A-Z or a-z. Case does not matter.
- Is the same whatever case is used. (EMP, Emp, and emp are all the same table.)
- May contain letters, numerals, and the underscore character (_). It may not contain a space.
- May be up to 30 characters in length.
- May not duplicate the name of another table or view.
- May not be an ORACLE reserved word such as SELECT, etc.

If you enclose a table name in double quotes ("), the first three rules listed on the last screen do not apply. The following two rules do apply:

- The name may contain any character except a double quote.
- Uppercase and lowercase letters are not equivalent. ("EMP, "Emp", and "emp" are different tables.)

Here are some examples of valid and invalid names:

NAME	VALIDITY
DEPT34	Valid
34DEPT	Invalid, begins with a number
TAX_LIABILITY	Valid
TAX LIABILITY	Invalid, contains a space
"TAX LIABILITY"	Valid, space permissible in double quotes
SELECT	Invalid, SQL reserved word
TEMP_TABLE	Valid, but use a more descriptive name. This name could be more descriptive, if it contained a reference to the contents of the table.

In the CREATE statement, the table name is followed by a list of information enclosed in parentheses. This consists of information about each column in the table to be created, separated by commas.

For each column specified, enter its name and data type. If null values (undefined or unknown values) are not allowed for values contained in a particular column, enter NOT NULL after the data type specification.

Here is how you specify the data types permissible in ORACLE in a CREATE TABLE statement:

DATA TYPE	DESCRIPTION
CHAR(n)	Character data, n characters long
VARCHAR(n)	Same as CHAR(n)
DATE	Date values
NUMBER	Numeric data, maximum width 40 digits, without decimal point and sign
NUMBER(n)	Numeric data, maximum width n digits
NUMBER(m,n)	Numeric data, m digits before decimal point, n digits after decimal point
DECIMAL	Same as NUMBER, cannot specify width or number of digits after decimal point

DATA TYPE	DESCRIPTION
FLOAT	Same as NUMBER
INTEGER	Same as DECIMAL
SMALLINT	Same as SMALLINT
LONG	Character data of variable size, up to 65,535 characters
LONG VARCHAR	Same as LONG
LONG RAW	Raw binary data
RAW(n)	Raw binary data, n bytes long. Maximum size 240 bytes

It is useful to forbid null values in columns when defining them in the CREATE TABLE statement. For example, every employee should have an employee number (EMPNO value in the EMP table). Therefore, it is useful to enter NOT NULL after the EMPNO column specification in the CREATE TABLE statement.

Here is the CREATE TABLE statement for the EMP table:

```
CREATE TABLE EMP
        EMPNO NUMBER(4) NOT NULL,
        ENAME CHAR(10),
        JOB CHAR(9),
        MGR NUMBER(4),
        HIREDATE DATE
        SAL NUMBER(7,2),
        COMM NUMBER(7,2),
        DEPTNO NUMBER(2));
```

Once a table is created, use the INSERT command to add values to the table.

CREATE TABLE AS SELECT

Now let's look at an ORACLE variation on the standard SQL CREATE TABLE statement.

ORACLE provides an extension to standard SQL that allows you to create a new table and copy the result of a query into it in one easy step.

This form of CREATE TABLE has the following syntax:

```
CREATE TABLE <table_name>
[(<column_name_1> [NOT NULL],
  <column_name_2> [NOT NULL],
   ...              ...
  <column_name_n> [NOT NULL])]
AS [query];
```

For example, suppose you want to create a new table called LOWSALARIES that includes the first three salary grades from the SALGRADE table. You can create the table and insert data into it with the new form of CREATE TABLE:

```
CREATE TABLE LOWSALARIES (SALARYGRADE NOT NULL,
                          LOWERLIMIT NOT NULL,
                          UPPERLIMIT NOT NULL)
AS SELECT *
FROM SALGRADE
WHERE GRADE IN (1,2,3);
```

Notice in the new table LOWSALARIES, the SALGRADE table columns GRADE, LOSAL, and HISAL are called SALARYGRADE, LOWERLIMIT, and UPPERLIMIT, respectively. Each column in the new table has been specified as not allowing NULL values (NOT NULL). NOT NULL is optional in the CREATE QUERY ... AS SELECT format.

Notice also that no datatype is specified for the columns in the new table. The columns in the new table assume the datatype of the columns from which they receive data.

Here is what the new table LOWSALARIES looks like:

```
SELECT *
FROM LOWSALARIES;
```

This displays the result:

```
SALARYGRADE  LOWERLIMIT  UPPERLIMIT
-----------  ----------  ----------
          1         700        1200
          2        1201        1400
          3        1401        2000
```

The specification of column names in a table created with the CREATE TABLE ... AS SELECT is not necessary. If column names are not specified, the column names in the new table assume the names of the columns in the table from which they are receiving data.

Here is the syntax of CREATE TABLE ... AS SELECT without the column specifications:

```
CREATE TABLE <table_name>
AS [query];
```

For example, suppose you want to give bonuses to all the managers, along with other employees, whose commission is greater than 25% of their salary.

Create a new table BONUS2 from data that already exist in the EMP table.

You can create BONUS2 with the following SQL statement:

```
CREATE TABLE BONUS2
AS SELECT ENAME, JOB, SAL, COMM
FROM EMP
WHERE JOB = 'MANAGER'
OR COMM > 0.25 * SAL;
```

Notice that no column names were specified for BONUS2. The column names in BONUS2 are the names of the columns specified in the query—ENAME, JOB, SAL, and COMM.

Here is what the new table BONUS2 looks like:

```
SELECT *
FROM BONUS2;
```

This displays the following:

```
ENAME       JOB            SAL     COMM
----------  ---------  -------  -------
WARD        SALESMAN      1250      500
JONES       MANAGER       2975
MARTIN      SALESMAN      1250     1400
BLAKE       MANAGER       2850
CLARK       MANAGER       2450
```

DESCRIBE

If you want to check the structure of new tables, use the DESCRIBE command. DESCRIBE is not a standard SQL command, but an extension of standard SQL provided by ORACLE. DESCRIBE displays a brief description of a specified table and has the following syntax:

```
DESC[RIBE] [<user_name>.] <table_name>;
```

Note that you can use the abbreviation DESC instead of the entire word DESCRIBE. You only need to use the "<user_name>." prefix if you are describing another user's table.

Suppose you want to check the structure of the two new tables LOWSALARIES and BONUS2. First, type:

```
DESCRIBE LOWSALARIES;
```

Here is the result:

```
Name                             Null?     Type
-------------------------------  --------  ----
SALARYGRADE                      NOT NULL  NUMBER
LOWERLIMIT                       NOT NULL  NUMBER
UPPERLIMIT                       NOT NULL  NUMBER
```

Notice that the table that results from the use of DESCRIBE contains a row for each column specified in the CREATE TABLE statement. Each row contains the name of the column (Name), whether or not it accepts null values (Null?), and its data type (Type). If a column accepts null values, the Null? column contains the value NOT NULL.

```
Name                               Null?     Type
------------------------------- -------- ----
SALARYGRADE                        NOT NULL  NUMBER
LOWERLIMIT                         NOT NULL  NUMBER
UPPERLIMIT                         NOT NULL  NUMBER
```

Because the CREATE TABLE ... AS SELECT command was used to create the LOWSALARIES table, the three columns in this table inherit their column descriptions from the SALGRADE table. Thus, the SALARYGRADE, LOWERLIMIT, and UPPERLIMIT columns have the same Null? and Type values as the GRADE, LOSAL, and HISAL columns in the SALGRADE table.

If you use DESCRIBE on the BONUS2 table as follows

```
DESCRIBE BONUS2;
```

you see the results:

```
Name                               Null?     Type
------------------------------- -------- ----
ENAME                                        CHAR(10)
JOB                                          CHAR(9)
SAL                                          NUMBER(7,2)
COMM                                         NUMBER(7,2)
```

The ENAME, JOB, SAL, and COMM columns in the BONUS2 columns have the same Null? and Type values as their counterparts in the EMP table.

USING DICTIONARY TABLES TO REVIEW WORK

Using the DESCRIBE command is one way to review the work you have done on tables. Another method is to use tables from the data dictionary.

The data dictionary is a group of tables and views that contain information about the database. These tables are created when the tables and other items in the database are created. These dictionary tables are modified whenever there is a change in a table for which they contain information.

Dictionary tables (those in the data dictionary) can be queried with standard SQL queries. This is useful when you need information about a table or another database item such as a column, index, user, or privilege.

One of the tables contained in the data dictionary is the CATALOG table. The CATALOG table contains information on all tables and views that the current user has created or has access to.

Some of the useful columns in the CATALOG table are TNAME (table name), CREATOR (user identification of the creator of the table), and TABLETYPE (indicates whether a table is a TABLE, VIEW, or SYNONYM). CATALOG also contains several other columns.

For a complete list of columns in CATALOG, see the SQL*Plus Reference Guide.

Suppose you want to know the creator and table type of the BONUS2 table. Use the following query of the dictionary table CATALOG to find out:

```
SELECT TNAME, CREATOR, TABLETYPE
FROM CATALOG WHERE
TNAME = 'BONUS2';
```

Here are the results for user SCOTT:

```
TNAME       CREATOR       TABLETY
---------   ------------  -------
BONUS2      SCOTT         TABLE
```

Here the creator's user identification is SCOTT, and the table is table, not a view or synonym (TABLETYPE value is TABLE).

Another dictionary table that you may find useful is the TAB table. TAB is a smaller version of the CATALOG table. Only the columns TNAME (table name), TABTYPE (table type), and CLUSTERID are presented.

Querying TAB is a useful shortcut to querying CATALOG, if you do not need all the information included in the latter table.

To see all of the tables you have created or have access to, execute the following query:

```
SELECT * FROM TAB;
```

Here is a possible result:

```
TNAME                            TABTYPE  CLUSTERID
------------------------------   -------  ---------
BONUS                            TABLE
BONUS2                           TABLE
DAN                              TABLE
DEPT                             TABLE
EA                               SYNONYM
EMP                              TABLE
EMP_ADDR                         TABLE
EMP_SAL                          TABLE
LOWSALARIES                      TABLE
SALGRADE                         TABLE
SALHIST                          TABLE
SALHISTORY                       TABLE
TEMP1                            TABLE
TEST                             TABLE
```

Another useful dictionary table is COLUMNS. COLUMNS contains information on the columns of tables that are accessible to the current user, including the tables the current user has created.

Some of the useful columns in the COLUMNS table are:

- CNAME (column name)
- TNAME (table that table is part of)
- CREATOR (creator of table containing column)
- COLTYPE (data type of column as specified in CREATE TABLE statement)
- WIDTH (how many digits or characters a column holds)
- NULLS (NULL if null values are permitted, NOT NULL if they are not)

Remember how you used DESCRIBE to find out column names, whether nulls were permitted for the column, and data types for columns in LOWSALARIES and BONUS2?

You can find out the same information by querying the COLUMNS dictionary table.

If you want to know information about the columns contained in the BONUS2 table, execute the following query:

```
SELECT CNAME, TNAME, COLTYPE, WIDTH, NULLS
FROM COLUMNS
WHERE TNAME = 'BONUS2';
```

Here is the result, which shows you the column names (CNAME), table name (TNAME), data types (COLTYPE), width (WIDTH), and whether null values are permissible (NULLS) for the columns in the BONUS2 table:

```
CNAME       TNAME       COLTYP    WIDTH  NULLS
----------  ----------  ------  -------  --------
ENAME       BONUS2      CHAR         10  NULL
JOB         BONUS2      CHAR          9  NULL
SAL         BONUS2      NUMBER        7  NULL
COMM        BONUS2      NUMBER        7  NULL
```

The dictionary table COL is identical to the COLUMNS table, with two exceptions:

1. The CREATOR column is not included.
2. Only columns in tables created by the current user are included in COL.

COL is useful if you want to list only those tables that you created.

COMMENT ON

One column that is included in the CATALOG, COLUMNS, and COL dictionary tables is the REMARKS column. This column contains descriptions of tables or columns created by the user.

These remarks are created with the COMMENT ON command.

Here is the syntax for creating a comment on a table:

```
COMMENT ON TABLE <table_name> IS 'character_string'
```

You do not have to specify which dictionary table in which to include the comment. The system automatically inserts the comments into the appropriate tables.

Suppose you want to create a comment on the BONUS2 table that reads 'employees eligible for bonuses'. Enter this command:

```
COMMENT ON TABLE BONUS2 IS
'employees eligible for bonuses';
```

The message "Comment created" appears.

When you want to see the comment created for the BONUS2 table, execute the following query of the CATALOG table:

```
SELECT REMARKS FROM CATALOG
WHERE TNAME = 'BONUS2';
```

Here is the result:

```
REMARKS
--------------------------------------------------------------
employees eligible for bonuses
```

You will not see the comment by querying the TAB table, because TAB does not contain the REMARKS column. Furthermore, if you display the REMARKS column from either the COLUMNS or COL tables, you do not see this particular comment. The comments contained in those tables relate to column names, not table names.

Let's create a comment on one of the columns in the LOWSALARIES table. To create a description of the LOWERLIMIT column that reads 'lower limit of this salary grade', enter the following SQL statement:

```
COMMENT ON COLUMN LOWSALARIES.LOWERLIMIT IS
'lower limit of this salary grade';
```

Notice that you need to qualify the LOWERLIMIT column with the name of the table in which it is contained, LOWSALARIES.

Again, the message "Comment created" appears.

In the future, you can execute this query to display the description of the LOWERLIMIT column:

```
SELECT REMARKS
FROM COLUMNS
WHERE CNAME = 'LOWERLIMIT';
```

Here is the result:

```
REMARKS
--------------------------------------------------------------
lower limit of this salary grade
```

You see the same result if you query the COL table because the comment is inserted by the system into all applicable dictionary tables.

ALTER TABLE

Now let's look at how to modify tables once they are created.

The standard SQL command ALTER TABLE allows you to add a column to an existing table. Here is the syntax:

```
ALTER TABLE <table_name>
ADD (<column_name> <datatype> [NOT NULL]);
```

The table must be empty for you to specify NOT NULL as the new column's data type. Otherwise, the new column must accept null values because existing rows will have null as the value of the new column.

For example, if you want to add a column called HIREDATE of the DATE data type to the BONUS2 table, you can execute the following SQL statement:

```
ALTER TABLE BONUS2
ADD (HIREDATE DATE);
```

The "Table altered" message appears.

If you display the BONUS2 table with this query:

```
SELECT * FROM BONUS2;
```

you see the table with the HIREDATE column added to it:

```
ENAME       JOB          SAL      COMM  HIREDATE
----------  ---------  -------  -------  ---------
WARD        SALESMAN      1250      500
JONES       MANAGER       2975
MARTIN      SALESMAN      1250     1400
BLAKE       MANAGER       2850
CLARK       MANAGER       2450
```

To add values to the HIREDATE column of BONUS2, you need to use the INSERT command.

ORACLE offers an extension to standard SQL that allows you to modify the specifications of existing columns. This is done with a form of ALTER TABLE (normally used to add columns to an existing table):

```
ALTER TABLE <table_name>
MODIFY (<column_name> <data_type> [NOT NULL]);
```

You can always increase a column's width or change its number of decimal places. You can decrease a column's width or change its data type only if there are no non-null values in the column.

If the table to be modified is empty, the table can be modified in any way. But, if the table contains data, you may not be able to specify NOT NULL for the new table. If a column to be modified contains null values, you cannot specify NOT NULL in the ALTER TABLE ... MODIFY statement.

Let's look at an example. In the original definition of the EMP table, the specification of the ENAME column is CHAR(10). This means that the maximum number of characters allowed in the ENAME field is 10.

Suppose a new employee named Sherwood-Forrest has been hired. Because this name has 16 characters, it will not fit in the ENAME field.

Use the ALTER TABLE ... MODIFY command to change the width of ENAME:

```
ALTER TABLE EMP
MODIFY (ENAME CHAR(20) NULL);
```

The "Table altered" message appears. The ENAME column can now accommodate names of up to 20 characters long.

In this chapter, you learned how to:

- Create tables with the CREATE TABLE command
- Use CREATE TABLE SELECT AS, the ORACLE extension to CREATE TABLE
- Check the structure of your tables with DESCRIBE
- Use data dictionary tables as an alternative to DESCRIBE
- Create remarks with COMMENT ON
- Modify tables with ALTER TABLE

Let's look at some workshop exercises to practice these concepts.

Workshop Exercises

Tables

In this section, you will practice the following concepts:

1. The use of CREATE TABLE
2. The use of ORACLE's data dictionary tables
3. The use of ORACLE's DESCRIBE feature
4. The use of ALTER TABLE

Let's review the creation of tables and see how to find and use information about the tables in the ORACLE catalog.

Exercise 7.1

Let's add a new table to our database to track salary history. Name the table SALHIST and give it four columns:

- EMPNO as a four-digit number that may not be NULL
- FROMDATE as a date that may not be NULL
- TODATE as a date that may be NULL
- SAL as a seven-digit number with two decimals that may not be NULL

RESULT:

```
Table created.
```

Write your answer here:

Exercise 7.2

ORACLE allows another useful variation on standard SQL. You can CREATE a new table and load it in one step by adding a query preceded by AS, like this:

```
CREATE TABLE ...
(col-id-1, col-id-2,... )
  AS SELECT EMPNO, HIREDATE, NULL, SAL
  FROM EMP;
```

Note that data types are omitted from the column list in the format above.

For this exercise, issue a DROP TABLE SALHIST statement, then re-create the table and load its data for all CLERKs in the EMP table. List the contents of the new table.

RESULT:

```
Table dropped.
Table created.

 EMPNO     FROMDATE      T          SAL
 -----     ---------     -----     ----
 7369      17-DEC-80                800
 7876      12-JAN-83               1100
 7900      03-DEC-81                950
 7934      23-JAN-82               1300
```

Write your answer here:

____

____

____

____

____

____

Exercise 7.3

We can see the data in the table by using a SELECT statement. How can we see information about the table? For this exercise, SELECT a row from the system table "CATALOG." Use a predicate, choosing rows in which the TNAME column has the value 'SALHIST.'

RESULT:

```
TNAME    CREATOR TABLETY CLUSTERID LOGBLK REQBLK IXCOMP  REMARKS
-------  ------- ------- --------- ------ ------ ------  -------
SALHIST  BRUCE   TABLE                980
```

Write your answer here:

____

____

____

____

____

____

Exercise 7.4

Another view into the catalog is named TAB. Show all rows from TAB. (Note: If you have created other tables in your database, your result table will differ.)

RESULT:

```
TNAME       TABTYPE    CLUSTERID
--------    -------    ---------
BONUS       TABLE
DEPT        TABLE
EMP         TABLE
SALGRADE    TABLE
SALHIST     TABLE
```

Write your answer here:

Exercise 7.5

The catalog tables also keep information about which COLUMNS are in which tables. Find information for TNAME = 'SALHIST' from the view COLUMNS.

RESULT:

```
CNAME                          TNAME
------------------------------ ------------------------------
CREATOR                          COLNO  COLTYP     WIDTH    SCALE NULLS
------------------------------ ------- ------- ------- ------- --------
REMARKS
-----------------------------------------------------------------------
DEFAULTVAL
-----------------------------------------------------------------------
EMPNO                          SALHIST
BRUCE                                1 NUMBER        4        0 NOT NULL

FROMDATE                       SALHIST
BRUCE                                2 DATE          7          NOT NULL

TODATE                         SALHIST
BRUCE                                3 CHAR          0          NULL

SAL                            SALHIST
BRUCE                                4 NUMBER        7        2 NOT NULL
```

Write your answer here:

Exercise 7.6

When you need to look at information about columns, ORACLE provides a shortcut for users. Show all the rows in the dictionary view COL. (Note: If you have created other tables in your database, your result table will differ.)

RESULT:

TNAME	CNAME	COLTYP
BONUS	ENAME	CHAR
BONUS	JOB	CHAR
BONUS	SAL	NUMBER
BONUS	COMM	NUMBER
DEPT	DEPTNO	NUMBER
DEPT	DNAME	CHAR
DEPT	LOC	CHAR
EMP	EMPNO	NUMBER
EMP	ENAME	CHAR
EMP	JOB	CHAR
EMP	MGR	NUMBER
EMP	HIREDATE	DATE
EMP	SAL	NUMBER
EMP	COMM	NUMBER
EMP	DEPTNO	NUMBER
SALGRADE	GRADE	NUMBER
SALGRADE	LOSAL	NUMBER
SALGRADE	HISAL	NUMBER
SALHIST	EMPNO	NUMBER
SALHIST	FROMDATE	DATE
SALHIST	TODATE	CHAR
SALHIST	SAL	NUMBER

Write your answer here:

____

____

____

____

____

____

Exercise 7.7

A useful shortcut allows you to see the information about one table's columns. Use ORACLE's SQL*Plus DESCRIBE command to find out about SALHIST.

RESULT:

```
Name                           Null?     Type
------------------------------ --------  ----
EMPNO                          NOT NULL  NUMBER(4)
FROMDATE                       NOT NULL  DATE
TODATE                                   CHAR(0)
SAL                            NOT NULL  NUMBER(7,2)
```

Write your answer here:

____

____

____

____

____

____

Exercise 7.8

You can add remarks to a table's row in CATALOG and you may also add remarks for each column's row in COLUMNS. Use the SQL statement COMMENT ON TABLE to add a remark for SALHIST, and COMMENT ON COLUMN to annotate the FROMDATE column. Show the information for just those rows from the dictionary.

RESULT:

```
Comment created.
Comment created.

TNAME
------------------------------
REMARKS
--------------------------------------------------------------

SALHIST       record of salaries

TNAME                          CNAME
------------------------------ ------------------------------
REMARKS
--------------------------------------------------------------

SALHIST                        FROMDATE
date salary is effective
```

Write your answer here:

____

____

____

____

____

____

Exercise 7.9

All standard SQL systems permit the ALTER table statement. Add a new column to SALHIST named MGR as a four-digit number permitting nulls. List the revised table.

RESULT:

```
Table altered.

EMPNO     FROMDATE    T      SAL          MGR
-----     ---------   -      ----      -------
 7369     17-DEC-80           800
 7876     12-JAN-83          1100
 7900     03-DEC-81           950
 7934      3-JAN-82          1300
                                        (new column is NULL)
```

Write your answer here:

____

____

____

____

____

____

To practice working with tables in a simulated SQL environment, choose Menu Item 3 from Exercise Disk 2.

Solutions to Workshop Exercises

Exercise 7.1 - Solution

```
CREATE TABLE SALHIST (
EMPNO NUMBER(4) NOT NULL,
FROMDATE DATE NOT NULL,
TODATE DATE,
SAL NUMBER(7,2) NOT NULL);
```

Notes

Here's a quick review of the SQL CREATE TABLE statement. After the two keywords CREATE TABLE the new table is named; in this case, the name is SALHIST.

Inside the parentheses we name each of the columns in the table along with the column's data type and "nullability." ORACLE permits NULL or NOT NULL, with NULL as the default. Standard SQL also has NULL as the default, but does not allow the term NULL.

Each of these column specifications is separated with a comma, and the list is closed with a parenthesis.

Exercise 7.2 - Solution

```
DROP TABLE SALHIST;

CREATE TABLE SALHIST (
EMPNO NOT NULL, FROMDATE NOT NULL,
TODATE, SAL NOT NULL)
  AS SELECT EMPNO, HIREDATE, NULL, SAL
  FROM EMP WHERE JOB = 'CLERK';

SELECT * FROM SALHIST;
```

Notes

This special ORACLE format of CREATE TABLE uses a few rules that you must keep in mind.

1. Do not include data types in the column list after the table name. In this format, the data types are defined in the expressions in the SELECT clause of the subselect.

2. You may specify the NULL or NOT NULL options for each new column named. This is useful if you want the new table's columns to have different nullability from the original table's columns.
3. Omit the entire column list if the following are true:

   - All the expressions in the subselect's SELECT clause are simple column names.
   - You want the new table to have those same column names and nullability.

4. The AS SELECT... subquery must contain an equal number of expressions in its SELECT clause as the new table has columns.

   To make a copy of TAB1 in new TAB2 issue:

```
CREATE TABLE TAB1 AS SELECT * FROM TAB2;
```

Remember that this "AS SELECT..." feature of CREATE TABLE is not in standard SQL. Using SQL, copy this table in two steps:

1. Create the table with full column specifications:

```
CREATE TABLE SALHIST (
EMPNO SMALLINT ...);
```

2. Insert rows into the table using INSERT format 2:

```
INSERT INTO SALHIST
(EMPNO, FROMDATE, TODATE, SAL)
SELECT EMPNO, HIREDATE, NULL, SAL
FROM EMP WHERE JOB = 'CLERK';
```

Exercise 7.3 - Solution

```
SELECT * FROM CATALOG WHERE TNAME = 'SALHIST';
```

Notes

Each CREATE TABLE statement results in ORACLE's placing a new row into the system dictionary. This row is visible to you through a view named CATALOG. (Other SQL systems may call the table SYSTABLES.)

Among other information about this table in addition to its name is:

CREATOR	The USERID who issued the CREATE.
TABLETYPE	The type of table: TABLE, VIEW or SYNONYM.
CLUSTERID	Which CLUSTER the table belongs to, if any.
REMARKS	Comments stored with the COMMENT ON SQL statement.

If you issue the statement:

```
SELECT * FROM CATALOG WHERE CREATOR = USER;
```

you get all the rows that contain your connect ID in the CREATOR column. That is what USER means: the value of your connect ID.

Note that SQL*Plus can tell you what your connect ID is with:

```
SHOW USER;
```

This returns:

```
user is "BRUCE"
```

for a user with the ID of BRUCE.

In standard SQL you can query a small table to find USER:

```
SELECT USER FROM DEPT;
```

This results in:

```
USER
------
BRUCE   ← repeated for each row in the small table
BRUCE
BRUCE
```

Exercise 7.4 - Solution

```
SELECT * FROM TAB;
```

Notes

TAB views part of the CATALOG table row for those rows with CREATOR = USER. Only columns TNAME, TABTYPE, and CLUSTERID are presented to you. It's a quick shortcut and a good query for end-users. (By the way, your list may be different from the author's list—SQL allows for a dynamic, changing system.)

Exercise 7.5 - Solution

```
SELECT * FROM COLUMNS WHERE TNAME = 'SALHIST';
```

Notes

Again we have wide rows of data with many columns of information including:

COLTYPE	The data type of the column.
WIDTH	How many digits or characters it holds.
SCALE	For numbers, how many decimal places.
NULLS	Whether or not NULLS are permitted.

There is also a sequencing column in COLUMNS named COLNO. It has a 1, 2, 3, etc., for the first, second, third, etc., column in the order in which the columns were specified in the CREATE TABLE statement.

You can use the SELECT statement to show the columns in any sequence across the page, and in any ORDER BY sequence.

As you look at the data, notice a problem with the TODATE column: It was created as CHAR(0) instead of DATE. That's because of how we used the second format of the CREATE TABLE...AS SELECT in example Exercise 7.2:

```
CREATE TABLE SALHIST (
EMPNO NOT NULL, FROMDATE NOT NULL,
TODATE, SAL NOT NULL)
  AS SELECT EMPNO, HIREDATE, NULL, SAL
  FROM EMP WHERE JOB = 'CLERK';
```

We included NULL in our SELECT clause. ORACLE used CHAR(0) as the default column data type. To correct this we could DROP TABLE SALHIST and then start our saved query, CRSALH, to re-create SALHIST. The table could be loaded with an INSERT as shown in the notes of example Exercise 7.2.

Exercise 7.6 - Solution

```
SELECT TNAME, CNAME, COLTYPE FROM COL;
```

Notes

The view COL limits the rows selected to those rows from COLUMNS where CREATOR = USER. The CREATOR column is not part of COL.

We could limit the display by asking for only rows WHERE TNAME LIKE 'SAL%.' Then we should find only rows describing the SALGRADE and SALHIST columns.

Make your own views on top of the standard ORACLE views to show only the columns you usually need to see.

Exercise 7.7 - Solution

```
DESCRIBE SALHIST;
```

Notes

This is a nicely formatted display, but it lacks some of the data found in COLUMNS or COL. SQL*Plus allows you to DESCRIBE more than one table at a time:

```
DESCRIBE SALHIST, SALGRADE;
```

The resulting display does not differentiate between the columns from each of the tables. Use COL or COLUMNS if you need more data about multiple tables' columns.

Exercise 7.8 - Solution

```
COMMENT ON TABLE SALHIST IS 'record of salaries';

COMMENT ON COLUMN SALHIST.FROMDATE IS
'date salary is effective';

SELECT TNAME,REMARKS FROM CATALOG
WHERE TNAME = 'SALHIST';

SELECT TNAME, CNAME, REMARKS FROM COLUMNS
WHERE TNAME = 'SALHIST'
AND CNAME = 'FROMDATE';
```

Notes

We usually try to use COMMENT ON TABLE and COMMENT ON COLUMN as part of our normal documentation effort. Because tables frequently need to be re-created or revised, it's best to include all of the related data definition language (DDL) statements with the CREATE TABLE statement in a file. Those DDL statements would include CREATE VIEW, CREATE SYNONYM, COMMENT ON, and sometimes the security GRANT statements.

Exercise 7.9 - Solution

```
ALTER TABLE SALHIST ADD
(MGR NUMBER(4) NULL);
SELECT * FROM SALHIST;
```

Notes

The new column must permit NULLs once there is some data in the table. If the table were still empty, NOT NULL would be allowed.

The new column is always added to the right of existing columns in the table. It is given the next higher COLNO in COLUMNS and COL. List CNAME, COLNO, and COLTYPE for this table from COL to check this out.

Once a new column is added, you cannot remove it directly. Indirectly you can unload your table (to another temporary table or to an external file), DROP the table, then re-CREATE the table without the undesired column.

8

Views

This chapter deals with advanced uses of views, which are "windows" on base tables that allow users to see selected portions of a database.

The use of views to INSERT, UPDATE, and DELETE data from base tables is discussed.

REVIEW OF VIEWS

Views are "windows" that allow users to see selected portions of a database. Views are also known as virtual tables because they contain no data of their own. The view tables themselves are not stored, only their definitions.

A view may be used to:

- Display portions of one or more tables
- Display portions of combinations of views and tables
- Add, update, insert, and delete table rows

Although views contain no data of their own, they appear as normal tables with columns and rows.

Views serve two primary purposes:

- Simplifying data access
- Enhancing data security

The syntax for creating a view is:

```
CREATE VIEW <view_name>
[(view_column_1, ...)]
AS <SQL query statements>;
```

Because the result of a query is itself a table, a query is used to define a view.

Suppose you want to maintain a list of salespeople and their hiring dates. Enter this SQL query:

```
SELECT ENAME, HIREDATE
FROM EMP
WHERE JOB = 'SALESMAN';
```

If you need this information frequently, here is an easy strategy. Create a view called SALESHIRE that contains the desired information. This speeds up retrieval of the names and hiring dates of salespeople:

```
CREATE VIEW SALESHIRE
AS SELECT ENAME, HIREDATE
FROM EMP
WHERE JOB = 'SALESMAN';
```

Note that when this view is created, the name 'SALESHIRE' is provided. Then the contents of the view are described as a query, SELECT ENAME, HIREDATE FROM EMP WHERE JOB = 'SALESMAN'. This query is saved by the RDBMS as the view's definition.

The view SALESHIRE can be queried as if it were an actual table.

```
SELECT *
FROM SALESHIRE;
```

This displays the desired information about salespeople:

```
ENAME       HIREDATE
----------  ---------
ALLEN       20-FEB-81
WARD        22-FEB-81
MARTIN      28-SEP-81
TURNER      08-SEP-81
```

When the view SALESHIRE is queried, its query definition is retrieved and executed.

You do not have to use the column names of the table being viewed as the column names of your view table. If you want to call the ENAME column SALESMAN and the HIREDATE column HIRED, you can define your view in this manner:

```
CREATE VIEW SALESHIRE (SALESMAN, HIRED)
AS SELECT ENAME, HIREDATE
FROM EMP
WHERE JOB = 'SALESMAN';
```

Make sure that the order in which you list the new column names corresponds to their counterparts in the SELECT clause.

Execute the query:

```
SELECT *
FROM SALESHIRE;
```

This displays this result:

```
ENAME        HIREDATE
----------   ---------
ALLEN        20-FEB-81
WARD         22-FEB-81
MARTIN       28-SEP-81
TURNER       08-SEP-81
```

You can use a WHERE clause with a query against a view. For example, you can enter the following query of SALESHIRE to display salespeople who were hired after February 22, 1981:

```
SELECT *
FROM SALESHIRE
WHERE HIREDATE > '22-FEB-81';
```

How does the WHERE clause of the query against the view interact with the WHERE clause of the query used in the original view definition?

The condition in the WHERE clause of the query against the view (HIREDATE > '22-FEB-81') is added to the query that is the original view definition in this fashion:

```
SELECT ENAME
FROM EMP
WHERE JOB = 'SALESMAN'
AND HIREDATE > '22-FEB-81';
```

Here is the query against the view:

```
SELECT *
FROM SALESHIRE
WHERE HIREDATE > '22-FEB-81';
```

This appears as:

```
SALESMAN  HIRED
--------  ---------
MARTIN    28-SEP-81
TURNER    08-SEP-81
```

VIEWS WITH COMPLEX QUERIES

As mentioned, an important advantage of the view feature is simplified data access. Complex queries can be defined as a view. The view can be easily and accurately queried in the future.

For example, you might want to create a view that is defined as a query on two tables (without a join) that includes a subquery.

Suppose you want to list employee names, jobs, and department numbers of those employees who work in New York. Because employee names are stored in the EMP table and department names are stored in the DEPT table, this query requires the use of two tables. A subquery on the DEPT table is used to find the department number(s) of those employees in New York:

```
SELECT ENAME, JOB, DEPTNO
FROM EMP
WHERE DEPTNO =
(SELECT DEPTNO FROM DEPT
WHERE LOC = 'NEW YORK');
```

Rather than enter this complex query every time you need to retrieve the information about employees in New York, you can use the query to define a view called NY_EMP:

```
CREATE VIEW NY_EMP
AS SELECT ENAME, JOB, DEPTNO
FROM EMP
WHERE DEPTNO =
(SELECT DEPTNO FROM DEPT
WHERE LOC = 'NEW YORK');
```

You can now query this view with the SQL statement:

```
SELECT *
FROM NY_EMP;
```

Here are the results:

```
ENAME      JOB        DEPTNO
---------- ---------  -------
CLARK      MANAGER         10
KING       PRESIDENT       10
MILLER     CLERK           10
```

Querying the view saves time and ensures accuracy.

You can also include joins in a view's definition. You are not limited to two tables when you define a view as a join. For example, suppose you want a list of employee names, their department names, and their salary grades. Employee names are in the EMP table, and salary grades are in the SALGRADE table. Therefore, three tables must be joined.

Here is the query that is necessary for this three-table join:

```
SELECT E.ENAME, D.DNAME, S.GRADE
FROM EMP E, DEPT D, SALGRADE S
WHERE E.DEPTNO = D.DEPTNO
AND E.SAL BETWEEN S.LOSAL AND S.HISAL;
```

This is a complex query involving two join predicates (conditions). Entering this accurately could be time consuming.

The solution is to define this three-table join as a view, called NAME_GRADE. In the future, you can query the view.

Here is the view definition:

```
CREATE VIEW NAME_GRADE
AS SELECT E.ENAME, D.DNAME, S.GRADE
FROM EMP E, DEPT D, SALGRADE S
WHERE E.DEPTNO = D.DEPTNO
AND E.SAL BETWEEN S.LOSAL AND S.HISAL;
```

If this view is queried:

```
SELECT *
FROM NAME_GRADE;
```

the following table results.

```
ENAME       DNAME            GRADE
----------  ---------------  -------
MILLER      ACCOUNTING             2
KING        ACCOUNTING             5
CLARK       ACCOUNTING             4
SMITH       RESEARCH               1
SCOTT       RESEARCH               4
JONES       RESEARCH               4
ADAMS       RESEARCH               1
FORD        RESEARCH               4
JAMES       SALES                  1
BLAKE       SALES                  4
TURNER      SALES                  3
MARTIN      SALES                  2
ALLEN       SALES                  3
WARD        SALES                  2
```

Now, if you want to know the salary grades of all the employees in the Accounting Department, enter this query of NAME_GRADE:

```
SELECT *
FROM NAME_GRADE
WHERE DNAME = 'ACCOUNTING';
```

Here is the result:

```
ENAME       DNAME            GRADE
----------  ---------------  -------
MILLER      ACCOUNTING             2
KING        ACCOUNTING             5
CLARK       ACCOUNTING             4
```

MODIFYING DATA THROUGH VIEWS

You have seen that views can be queried with the SELECT statement as if they are tables. INSERT, UPDATE, and DELETE can also be used with views, although with some restrictions.

You can delete rows from a base table using a view if the query used to define the view:

- Selects rows from only one table
- Does not contain a GROUP BY clause, a DISTINCT clause, an aggregate (group) function, or a reference to the pseudo column ROWNUM.

You can update rows in a base table using a view if:

- The view meets the restrictions for deleting a row through a view, and
- The view does not define any of the update columns with an expression (one or more data items combined with operators or functions).

You can insert rows in a base table using a view if:

- The view meets the restrictions for deleting and updating through a view, and
- Any columns in the base table defined as NOT NULL (not accepting null values) must be included in the view.

When views do not meet these restrictions, they are read-only views and can only be queried.

Let's look at an example of deleting a row from a base table through a view.

Suppose that employee Allen, who is a salesman, has left the company. You want to delete information about Allen from the database.

One method is to delete Allen's record from the EMP table.

Another method is to remove Allen's record from the SALESHIRE table:

```
DELETE FROM SALESHIRE
WHERE SALESMAN = 'ALLEN';
```

If you query SALESHIRE, information on Allen is no longer there:

```
SELECT * FROM SALESHIRE;
```

This displays the following result:

```
SALESMAN     HIRED
----------   ---------
WARD         22-FEB-81
MARTIN       28-SEP-81
TURNER       08-SEP-81
```

Is the information on Allen still in the EMP table? No. When the information on Allen was deleted from the SALESHIRE view, it was also deleted from EMP, the table SALESHIRE was derived from.

Perform the following query on EMP:

```
SELECT *
FROM EMP
WHERE JOB = 'SALESMAN';
```

Allen's record is no longer there:

EMPNO	ENAME	JOB	MGR	HIREDATE	SAL	COMM	DEPTNO
7521	WARD	SALESMAN	7698	22-FEB-81	1250	500	30
7654	MARTIN	SALESMAN	7698	28-SEP-81	1250	1400	30
7844	TURNER	SALESMAN	7698	08-SEP-81	1500	0	30

What if you try to delete information on employee Clark? Can you use the NY_EMP table to delete Clark's record from the database?

Remember that the definition of the NY_EMP view is as follows:

```
CREATE VIEW NY_EMP
AS SELECT ENAME, JOB, DEPTNO
FROM EMP
WHERE DEPTNO =
(SELECT DEPTNO FROM DEPT
WHERE LOC = 'NEW YORK');
```

Two tables, EMP and DEPT, are involved in NY_EMP's definition. Does this violate the rule that a view can be used to delete records only if it selects rows from a single table? No, because the DEPT table is used only in the subquery. The rows that are selected are retrieved only from the EMP table.

The restriction against deleting rows from a view that selects rows from more than one table holds true if you try to delete rows from the NAME_GRADE view. Remember that NAME_GRADE was created with this SQL statement:

```
CREATE VIEW NAME_GRADE
AS SELECT E.ENAME, D.DNAME, S.GRADE
FROM EMP E, DEPT D, SALGRADE S
WHERE E.DEPTNO = D.DEPTNO
AND E.SAL BETWEEN S.LOSAL AND S.HISAL;
```


```
CREATE VIEW NAME_GRADE
AS SELECT E.ENAME, D.DNAME, S.GRADE
FROM EMP E, DEPT D, SALGRADE S
WHERE E.DEPTNO = D.DEPTNO
AND E.SAL BETWEEN S.LOSAL AND S.HISAL;
```


The query that was used to define NAME_GRADE is a join of three tables. Thus, the view NAME_GRADE selects rows from more than one table, and the

NAME_GRADE view cannot be used to delete rows from the database. If you attempt to delete rows from NAME_GRADE, an error message appears.

Because NAME_GRADE was created as a join of three tables, no INSERTs, UPDATEs, or DELETEs can be performed against it.

But UPDATEs can be performed against the SALESHIRE and NY_EMP views, because neither view selects rows from more than one table, and neither view contains a GROUP BY clause, a DISTINCT clause, an aggregate function, or a reference to ROWNUM. Finally, neither view has columns defined with an expression.

Let's look at an example of an UPDATE performed on the NY_EMP view.

Suppose that Clark, the manager of Department 10, has been named the manager of Department 40. Let's use an UPDATE of NY_EMP to make the change to the EMP table:

```
UPDATE NY_EMP
SET DEPTNO = 40
WHERE ENAME = 'CLARK';
```

The message "1 record updated." appears.

Let's see how this UPDATE has affected the NY_EMP view. If you list NY_EMP's contents:

```
SELECT *
FROM NY_EMP;
```

You see this table:

ENAME	JOB	DEPTNO
KING	PRESIDENT	10
MILLER	CLERK	10

Why does Clark no longer appear in the view? Remember that the query used to define NY_EMP retrieves only those employees working in New York, which means they work in Department 10. Once Clark's department number is changed, her record is no longer retrieved by the view.

But Clark's record has been updated. If we query EMP to look at Clark's record:

```
SELECT *
FROM EMP
WHERE JOB = 'MANAGER';
```

```
   EMPNO ENAME      JOB             MGR HIREDATE        SAL      COMM   DEPTNO
-------- ---------- --------- -------- --------- -------- -------- --------
    7566 JONES      MANAGER        7839 02-APR-81      2975                  20
    7698 BLAKE      MANAGER        7839 01-MAY-81      2850                  30
    7782 CLARK      MANAGER        7839 09-JUN-81      2450                  40
```

You see that Clark's new DEPTNO value is 40. Therefore, Clark's record was updated through the view, but her record is no longer displayed by the view.

There is an option to the CREATE VIEW syntax called WITH CHECK OPTION:

```
CREATE VIEW <view_name>
[(view_column_1, ...)]
AS <SQL query statements>
[WITH CHECK OPTION];
```

The WITH CHECK OPTION is used to ensure that INSERTs and UPDATEs performed through the view do not create rows that the view cannot select.

Both SALESHIRE and NY_EMP select rows from only one table, and neither definition of the views contains a DISTINCT clause, a group function, or a reference to ROWNUM. Neither view defines columns with expressions.

Can you insert rows into the base table EMP with the INSERT operation on SALESHIRE or NY_EMP?

No, because the EMPNO column, which was defined when EMP was created as a NOT NULL column, is not included in either view. Therefore, INSERTs cannot be performed on them. If you try to do so, an error message appears.

USING VIEWS TO ENHANCE SECURITY

You have seen that views simplify data access by storing complex queries as views, and by the manipulation of data through INSERT, UPDATE, and DELETE operations on views.

Views are also useful for enhancing data security.

Views provide an additional level of security by allowing you to create a view that contains only the information required by a user.

Suppose a client has requested a list of salespeople to contact for future purchases. Obviously, this client is not authorized to see the salary information of salespeople.

A view may be created listing only the names of salespeople.

Views can be used to:

- Select table columns

A view may be defined to contain only specific columns. Access to the view limits users to these columns only.

- Select table rows

A view may include only certain rows selected from a table or tables by using the WHERE and HAVING functions.

DROPPING VIEWS

Here is the syntax for dropping a view from the database:

```
DROP VIEW <view_name>;
```

If you want to remove the SALESHIRE view from the database, enter the following:

```
DROP VIEW SALESHIRE;
```

When you drop a view, views (and synonyms that refer to the view) are not dropped, but become invalid.

If a table is dropped, any views associated with the table are dropped as well.

Also, you cannot drop a view created by another user.

USING DICTIONARY TABLES TO EXAMINE VIEWS

In Lesson 7, "Tables," you saw that data dictionary tables can be used to review work on tables. Dictionary tables can also be used to examine views.

There is a dictionary table called VIEWS which contains information about views. VIEWS contains the names of views (VIEWNAME) and the text of the query used to create them (VIEWTEXT).

For example, if you enter the query of views:

```
SELECT *
FROM VIEWS
WHERE VIEWNAME = 'SALESHIRE';
```

You see this result:

```
VIEWNAME
------------------------------------
VIEWTEXT
------------------------------------
SALESHIRE
SELECT ENAME, HIREDATE
FROM EMP1
WHERE JOB = 'SALESMAN'
```

You can also query the CATALOG for information on views. Information on views is stored in the same manner as information on tables, but the column TABLETYPE contains the value 'VIEW'.

Similarly, the dictionary table TAB can be queried:

```
SELECT * FROM TAB
WHERE TABTYPE = 'VIEW';
```

Here are the results:

```
TNAME                             TABTYPE  CLUSTERID
--------------------------------  -------  ---------
NAME_GRADE                        VIEW
NY_EMP                            VIEW
SALESHIRE                         VIEW
```

Remember that you can use the DESCRIBE command to display a description of tables. You can also use DESCRIBE to list information on views in the database. If you use DESCRIBE on NAME_GRADE:

```
DESCRIBE NAME_GRADE;
```

you see:

```
Name                              Null?     Type
--------------------------------  --------  ----
ENAME                                       CHAR(10)
DNAME                                       CHAR(14)
GRADE                                       NUMBER
```

You see three things—the name of each column (Name), if it accepts null values (Null?), and the data type of each column (Type).

In this lesson, you learned how to:

- Use views with complex queries
- Modify data through views
- Enhance security with views
- Drop views
- Use dictionary tables to examine views

You can practice these concepts with the following workshop exercises.

Workshop Exercises

Views

In this section, you will practice the following concepts:

1. The use of CREATE VIEW
2. The use of ORACLE's data dictionary tables to review work
3. The use of ORACLE's DESCRIBE feature

In this section we are going to practice using views. Views are a very powerful feature of SQL systems. You will probably use views in all of your SQL projects.

Exercise 8.1

Let's add a simple view to our database. The view should be named "CLERKS."

The CLERKS view should contain all the columns from EMP for the employees who have the JOB of clerk. The names of the columns of the view should be the same as the names of the columns in EMP.

The result table shown below comes from a view into the ORACLE catalog called TAB.

RESULT:

```
View created.

TNAME        TABTYPE    CLUSTERID
--------     -------    ---------
BONUS        TABLE
CLERKS       VIEW
DEPT         TABLE
EMP          TABLE
SALGRADE     TABLE
```

Write your answer here:

____

____

____

____

____

____

Exercise 8.2

We'll change our mind, and give our view CLERKS different column names from the column names in EMP.

Issue a DROP VIEW statement and revise the view's column names to be the first four characters of the names from EMP. Use three characters for names already three characters long.

RESULT:

```
View dropped.
View created.
```

Write your answer here:

____

____

____

____

____

____

Exercise 8.3

Let's look at all the rows in our view. Issue a query and sort the results by the department column.

RESULT:

```
EMPN  ENAM    JOB    MGR   HIRE        SAL  COMM  DEPT
----  ------  -----  ----  ---------  ----  ----  ----
7934  MILLER  CLERK  7782  23-JAN-82  1300          10
7369  SMITH   CLERK  7902  17-DEC-80   800          20
7876  ADAMS   CLERK  7788  12-JAN-83  1100          20
7900  JAMES   CLERK  7698  03-DEC-81   950          30
```

Write your answer here:

____

____

____

____

____

____

Exercise 8.4

Use your CLERKS view to show all clerks earning less than $1000. Show only name, job, date hired, and salary.

RESULT:

```
ENAM    JOB     HIRE         SAL
-----   -----   ---------    ----
SMITH   CLERK   17-DEC-80    800
JAMES   CLERK   03-DEC-81    950
```

Write your answer here:

Exercise 8.5

There is a view into the catalog named VIEWS. Show all columns from VIEWS in which VIEWNAME = 'CLERKS'. Also DESCRIBE the view CLERKS and list your TAB rows again.

RESULT:

```
VIEWNAME
--------------------
VIEWTEXT
----------------------------------------------------
CLERKS    SELECT EMPNO, ENAME, JOB, MGR, HIREDATE, SAL, COMM, DEPTNO
FROM EMP WHERE JOB = 'CLERK'


Name     Null?        Type
----     --------     -----------
EMPN     NOT NULL     NUMBER(4)
ENAM                  CHAR(10)
JOB                   CHAR(9)
MGR                   NUMBER(4)
HIRE                  DATE
SAL                   NUMBER(7,2)
COMM                  NUMBER(7,2)
DEPT                  NUMBER(2)


TNAME        TABTYPE        CLUSTERID
--------     -----------    ---------
BONUS        TABLE
CLERKS       VIEW
DEPT         TABLE
EMP          TABLE
SALGRADE     TABLE
```

Write your answer here:

Exercise 8.6

Let's add a new row to our database using the CLERKS view. Use an INSERT with data 9991, CAMPBELL, ANALYST, 7566, 01-FEB-83, 2500, NULL, and 20. List the rows in CLERKS.

RESULT:

```
1 record created.

EMPN   ENAM     JOB     MGR    HIRE        SAL    COMM
----   ------   -----   ----   ---------   ----   ----
7934   MILLER   CLERK   7782   23-JAN-82   1300
7369   SMITH    CLERK   7902   17-DEC-80    800
7876   ADAMS    CLERK   7788   12-JAN-83   1100
7900   JAMES    CLERK   7698   03-DEC-81    950
```

Write your answer here:

____

____

____

____

____

____

Exercise 8.7

Let's add another view, "GRADES," which shows the GRADE, LOSAL, and HISAL columns from the SALGRADES table, and also shows a column "HEADCOUNT" with a count of employees in each GRADE. (Hint: You need to define a join with the BETWEEN predicate and form groups.)

RESULT:

```
View created.

GRADE     LOSAL     HISAL     HEADCOUNT
-----     -----     -----     ---------
    1       700      1200             3
    2      1201      1400             3
    3      1401      2000             2
    4      2001      3000             5
    5      3001      9999             1
```

Write your answer here:

Exercise 8.8

Let's add a new row of data through the view, GRADES. Use the data 9, 10000, 12000, 0 for the row.

RESULT:

```
INSERT INTO GRADES (GRADE, LOSAL, HISAL, HEADCOUNT)  VALUES
(9, 10000, 12000, 0)
*
ERROR at line 1:  ORA-1732:  data manipulation operation not
legal on this view
```

Write your answer here:

Exercise 8.9

As a final exercise, let's issue DROP VIEW statements for CLERKS and GRADES.

RESULT:

```
View dropped.
View dropped.
```

Write your answer here:

Excellent! You have completed the final workshop exercises. We hope you have enjoyed and benefited from the exercises in the workshop.

To practice using views in a simulated SQL environment, choose Menu Item 4 from Exercise Disk 2.

Solutions to Workshop Exercises

Exercise 8.1 - Solution

```
CREATE VIEW CLERKS
AS SELECT EMPNO, ENAME, JOB, MGR,
HIREDATE, SAL, COMM, DEPTNO
FROM EMP
WHERE JOB = 'CLERK';

SELECT * FROM TAB;
```

Notes

Each CREATE VIEW statement has two parts:

- The part that names the new view
- The section specifying how to build it with a SELECT statement called a subselect

The SELECT * form of the subselect, for example:

```
CREATE VIEW CLERKS
AS SELECT * FROM EMP
WHERE JOB = 'CLERK';
```

This subselect is permitted by ORACLE, but it is not recommended, especially because the table might receive a new column with an ALTER TABLE statement. We've shown the SELECT clause with an explicit list of the table's column names that correspond to the view's implied column names.

In this format of the SQL CREATE VIEW statement, we've omitted the view's column name list. If your subselect has simple column names (or the * as we've shown), then column names for the new view do not have to be specified.

We could have listed the column names, however, as in:

```
CREATE VIEW CLERKS (EMPNO, ENAME, JOB, MGR,
HIREDATE, SAL, COMM, DEPTNO)
AS SELECT EMPNO, ENAME, JOB, MGR,
HIREDATE, SAL, COMM, DEPTNO
FROM EMP
WHERE JOB = 'CLERK';
```

In our next exercise we'll discuss this format.

Exercise 8.2 - Solution

```
DROP VIEW CLERKS;

CREATE VIEW CLERKS
(EMPN, ENAM, JOB, MGR, HIRE, SAL, COMM, DEPT)
AS
  SELECT EMPNO, ENAME, JOB, MGR,
  HIREDATE, SAL, COMM, DEPTNO
  FROM EMP
  WHERE JOB = 'CLERK';
```

Notes

Each of the view's columns is named after the view's name. Be sure to place the column name list inside the parentheses.

When you explicitly name view columns, be careful to use the same number of expressions in the SELECT clause of the subselect.

Exercise 8.3 - Solution

```
SELECT * FROM CLERKS
ORDER BY DEPT;
```

Notes

Did you make an error and use DEPTNO in the ORDER BY clause? Once you refer to a view, you must use the view's column names.

We changed the table's column named DEPTNO to the view's column name DEPT in our attempt to have shorter column names. In fact, when you SELECT on this view, all clauses making any reference to the view's columns must now refer to EMPN, ENAM, JOB, MGR, HIRE, SAL, COMM, and DEPT.

Exercise 8.4 - Solution

```
SELECT ENAM, JOB, HIRE, SAL
FROM CLERKS WHERE SAL < 1000;
```

Notes

When you refer to a view, the system retrieves the definition of the view from its system dictionary tables. If you've added a WHERE clause as we have, the new WHERE clause predicates are AND-connected onto the definition's WHERE clause, as if the original WHERE clause were in parentheses, such as:

```
SELECT ENAME, JOB, HIREDATE, SAL
FROM EMP
WHERE (JOB = 'CLERK')
AND (SAL < 1000);
```

In this way the system prohibits you from violating the view by stating WHERE JOB = 'MANAGER', which would become the equivalent of:

```
SELECT ENAME, JOB, HIREDATE, SAL
FROM EMP
WHERE (JOB = 'CLERK')
AND (JOB = 'MANAGER');

"no records selected."
```

You can see that the AND means that no rows will be chosen because no row can contain both CLERK and MANAGER at the same time.

When the view is referenced in an SQL statement, the view's definition is retrieved from the dictionary. Notice that the column names and FROM clause refer to the original table:

```
SELECT ENAME, JOB, HIREDATE, SAL
FROM EMP
WHERE (JOB = 'CLERK')
AND (SAL < 1000);
```

Exercise 8.5 - Solution

```
SELECT * FROM VIEWS WHERE VIEWNAME = 'CLERKS';

DESCRIBE CLERKS;

SELECT * FROM TAB;
```

Notes

The VIEWS view shows the view definitions in a wide column named VIEWTEXT.

When you use a DESCRIBE command, the view's column names appear with the data types of the underlying table's column or expression.

In our TAB display, how is the row for CLERKS different from the other rows? The same information—that it is a view not a table or synonym—is found in the CATALOG from the ORACLE dictionary.

By using these dictionary queries and commands you will be able to find out about the views you own. (Views from other owners can't be found via the ORACLE CATALOG.)

Exercise 8.6 - Solution

```
INSERT INTO CLERKS
(EMPN, ENAM, JOB, MGR, HIRE, SAL, COMM, DEPT)
VALUES(9991, 'CAMPBELL', 'ANALYST',7566, '01-FEB-83', 2500, NULL, 20);
SELECT * FROM CLERKS;
```

Notes

Did you remember to list all of the view's column names after the name CLERKS? You would get an error if you listed the table's column names instead. Maybe you avoided the problem this time by omitting the column names, as in:

```
INSERT INTO CLERKS
VALUES(9991, 'CAMPBELL', 'ANALYST',7566,
'01-FEB-83', 2500, NULL, 20);
```

It's always best to list the column names explicitly instead of allowing the system to implicitly assign data to columns.

Was the new row in our list of rows from CLERKS? The system allowed the row to be inserted through the view. The view had no operators or clauses (such as AVG, GROUP BY, or DISTINCT) that would make it a read-only view.

However, the new row was not a "CLERK," so it disappeared from view when it was read from the table. Now list the underlying table and see if the row is there. It is.

The following query:

```
SELECT * FROM EMP WHERE JOB = 'ANALYST';
```

produces:

EMPNO	ENAME	JOB	MGR	HIREDATE	SAL	COMM
7788	SCOTT	ANALYST	7566	09-DEC-82	300	
7902	FORD	ANALYST	7566	03-DEC-81	3000	
9991	CAMPBELL	ANALYST	7566	01-FEB-83	2500	

To clean up the database, you would try both of the following:

```
DELETE FROM CLERKS WHERE EMPN > 9000;
```

and

```
DELETE FROM EMP WHERE EMPNO > 9000;
```

Which statement worked? Why didn't the DELETE work through the CLERKS view?

Exercise 8.7 - Solution

```
CREATE VIEW GRADES (GRADE, LOSAL, HISAL, HEADCOUNT)
AS SELECT S.GRADE, S.LOSAL, S.HISAL, COUNT(*)
FROM SALGRADE S, EMP E
WHERE E.SAL BETWEEN S.LOSAL AND S.HISAL
GROUP BY S.GRADE, S.LOSAL, S.HISAL;

SELECT * FROM GRADES;
```

Notes

In this example we've built a simple view for a complex query. This illustrates the usefulness of views.

The GROUP BY clause may have given you trouble if you did not use all three columns from SALGRADE to form each group. The query joins each row of EMP next to its corresponding SALGRADE row and then counts the rows in each group.

Exercise 8.8 - Solution

```
INSERT INTO GRADES (GRADE, LOSAL, HISAL, HEADCOUNT)
VALUES(9, 10000, 12000, 0);
```

Notes

Why didn't this insert work?

The view GRADES is a read-only view because the view contains two features that restrict us from updating it:

- It is formed from more than one table.
- It includes a GROUP BY clause.

Either of those reasons is sufficient to restrict update.

Exercise 8.9 - Solution

These statements solve Exercise 8.9:

```
DROP VIEW CLERKS;
DROP VIEW GRADES;
```

Notes

If the EMP table had been dropped, then any views defined on that table would have been automatically dropped as well.

These VIEW exercises have given you some experience working with this powerful relational feature.

A

Sample Tables

EMP

EMPNO	ENAME	JOB	MGR	HIREDATE	SAL	COMM	DEPTNO
7369	SMITH	CLERK	7902	17-DEC-1980	800		20
7499	ALLEN	SALESMAN	7698	20-FEB-1981	1600	300	30
7521	WARD	SALESMAN	7698	22-FEB-1981	1250	500	30
7566	JONES	MANAGER	7839	02-APR-1981	2975		20
7654	MARTIN	SALESMAN	7698	28-SEP-1981	1250	1400	30
7698	BLAKE	MANAGER	7839	01-MAY-1981	2850		30
7782	CLARK	MANAGER	7839	09-JUN-1981	2450		10
7788	SCOTT	ANALYST	7566	09-DEC-1982	3000		20
7839	KING	PRESIDENT		17-NOV-1981	5000		10
7844	TURNER	SALESMAN	7698	08-SEP-1981	1500	0	30
7876	ADAMS	CLERK	7788	12-JAN-1983	1100		20
7900	JAMES	CLERK	7698	03-DEC-1981	950		30
7902	FORD	ANALYST	7566	03-DEC-1981	3000		20
7934	MILLER	CLERK	7782	23-JAN-1982	1300		10

DEPT

DEPTNO	DNAME	LOC
10	ACCOUNTING	NEW YORK
20	RESEARCH	DALLAS
30	SALES	CHICAGO
40	OPERATIONS	BOSTON

BONUS

ENAME	JOB	SAL	COMM
SMITH	CLERK	800	
ALLEN	SALESMAN	1600	300
WARD	SALESMAN	1250	500
JONES	MANAGER	2975	
MARTIN	SALESMAN	1250	1400

SALGRADE

GRADE	LOSAL	HISAL
1	700	1200
2	1201	1400
3	1401	2000
4	2001	3000
5	3001	9999

B

Quick Syntax Reference

SELECT, the Basic Query Statement

```
SELECT [DISTINCT] <column-name(s) / * >
FROM <table-name>;
```

Ordering Rows

```
SELECT [DISTINCT] <column-name(s) / * >
FROM <table-name>
ORDER BY <column-name(s) / column-number(s)> [ASC / DESC];
```

Selecting Rows from a Table

```
SELECT <column-name(s)>
FROM <table-name>
WHERE <column-name> <comparison operator> <value>;
```

COMPARISON OPERATORS

=	equal to
<	less than
!=	not equal to
<=	less than or equal to
>	greater than
>=	greater than or equal to

Multiple Search Conditions

```
SELECT <column-name(s)>
FROM <table-name>
WHERE <condition> AND <condition>;
```

Alternate Search Conditions

```
SELECT <column-name(s)>
FROM <table-name>
WHERE <condition> OR <condition>;
```

Range Searches

```
SELECT <column-name(s)>
FROM <table-name>
WHERE <column-name>
[NOT] BETWEEN <value-1> AND <value-2>;

SELECT <column-name(s)>
FROM <table-name>
WHERE <value>
[NOT] BETWEEN <column-name-1> AND <column-name-2>;
```

Matching Character Patterns

```
SELECT <column-name(s)>
FROM <table-name>
WHERE <column-name>
[NOT] LIKE <'character string'>; Searching for Nulls

SELECT <column-name(s)>
FROM <table-name>
WHERE <column-name> IS [NOT] NULL;
```

Set Comparison Operators

```
SELECT <column-name(s)>
FROM <table-name>
WHERE <column-name>
[NOT] IN (<value-1>, <value-2>, ...);
```

Built-in Functions

```
SELECT built-in function([DISTINCT] <column-name>)
FROM <table-name>
[WHERE <condition>];
```

BUILT-IN FUNCTIONS:

```
AVG
SUM
MIN
MAX
COUNT      (may be used with *)
```

Calculations

```
SELECT <column-name(s)>, <arithmetic expression>
FROM <table-name>
[WHERE <condition>]
[ORDER BY <column-name(s) / * >];
```

ARITHMETIC OPERATORS

*	Multiplication
/	Division
+	Addition
-	Subtraction

Subqueries

Main Query

```
SELECT <column-name(s)>
FROM <table-name>
WHERE <comparison operator/set comparison operator>
```

Sub Query

```
(SELECT <column-name>
FROM <table-name>
[WHERE <condition>]);
```

Grouping

```
SELECT <column-name(s)>, <built-in function(argument)>
FROM <table-name>
[WHERE <condition>]
GROUP BY <column-name(s)>
[HAVING <condition>]
[ORDER BY <column-name(s) / column-number(s)> [ASC/DESC>]];
```

Joining Tables

```
SELECT <column-name(s)>
FROM <table-name>, <table-name> [, <table-name>, . . .]
WHERE <join-condition>
[AND / OR <condition>]
     [ORDER BY <column-name(s) / column-number(s)>];
```

Data Manipulation Language

```
INSERT INTO <table-name>
[(<column-name-1>, <column-name-2>, ...)]
VALUES (<value-1>, <value-2>, ...);

INSERT INTO <table-name>
[(<column-name-1, column-name-2, ...>)]
SELECT <column-name(s)>
FROM <table-name>
WHERE <condition>;

UPDATE <table-name / view-name>
SET <column-name-1> = <value / arithmetic expression>,
    ...              ...
    <column-name-n> = <value / arithmetic expression>
[WHERE <condition>];

DELETE FROM <table-name>
[WHERE <condition>];
```

Data Definition Language

```
CREATE TABLE <table-name>
(<column-name-1> <data-type> [NOT NULL],
 <column-name-2> <data-type> [NOT NULL],
  ...            ...         ...
 <column-name-n> <data-type> [NOT NULL]);
```

```
ALTER TABLE <table-name>
ADD <column-name> <data-type>;

DROP TABLE <table-name>;

CREATE [UNIQUE] INDEX <index-name>
ON <table-name> (<column-name(s)> [ASC / DESC]);

DROP INDEX (index-name);

CREATE SYNONYM <synonym-name>
FOR <table-name / view-name>;

DROP SYNONYM <synonym-name>;

CREATE VIEW <view-name>
AS <SQL query statements>;

DROP VIEW <view-name>;
```

Data Control Language

```
GRANT <ALL / SELECT / UPDATE / INSERT / DELETE / INDEX /
     ALTER>
ON <table-name(s) / view-name(s)>
TO <user-name(s)>;

REVOKE <ALL / SELECT / UPDATE / INSERT / DELETE / INDEX /
     ALTER>
ON <table-name(s) / view-name(s)>
FROM <user-name(s)>;
```

C

Glossary

alphanumeric Describes data that are made up of letters, numbers, or a combination of the two. Also may include characters such as periods and underscores.

application A computer program (software) designed to perform a specific task.

back end *See* database server.

catalog *See* system catalog.

column In a relation, or table, a column represents characteristics of entities. If the entities were employees, a column might contain employee numbers.

database An organized collection of information. A relational database is made up of several tables.

database management system (DBMS) Software used to create and access a database.

database server A database management system (DBMS) that is contained on a network server, a minicomputer, or a mainframe. Users access the DBMS from a PC or a terminal, through an interface known as the front end. The database server is also known as a back end or engine.

data control language Data control language commands grant and revoke privileges to access the database.

data definition language Data definition language commands allow the creation of database objects such as tables and views.

data dictionary *See* system catalog.

data manipulation language Data manipulation language commands are used to retrieve information from the database, remove information from the database, and add information to it.

data type The type of data that a column in a table may contain. Each column may contain data of only one type. Data types include character data, integer data, and decimal data. The data type of a column is defined when the table is created.

DBMS *See* database management system.

distributed database A database that is contained on several computers, but that appears to the user to be contained on a single computer.

engine *See* database server.

foreign key A primary key may be contained in more than one table, to reference a main table. It is known as a foreign key in the table that references the main table.

4GL (fourth-generation language) A language that lets a user specify what results are needed, rather than the actual steps required to get the result. SQL is a 4GL.

front end An interface. *See* database server.

GRANT An SQL keyword that permits the owner of a database object to grant privileges to other DBMS users. These privileges may include querying tables, inserting data into tables, updating, deleting, or altering tables.

join Rows in one table may be joined to rows in another by common values in corresponding columns. The result is a new table.

key *See* primary key, foreign key.

null An undefined value.

primary key The column in a relation, or table, whose values uniquely identify each row of the table. Each value in this column must be unique.

query A request for a display of information from tables. A query is carried out with the SELECT command.

query by example (QBE) An interface that lets a user enter an example of a result desired, rather than DBMS commands.

RDBMS A relational database management system.

record *See* row.

relation A two-dimensional table made up of rows and columns. Each table stores information about entities, such as employees, departments, etc. The columns in a table represent characteristics of entities, such as employee name, department number, etc. The rows in a table represent one occurrence, or record, of an employee, department, etc. Each row is made up of values, one for each column in the table. Each row must be unique. The primary key of a table is the column whose values uniquely identify each row of the table. For example, an employee number may uniquely identify rows in a table made up of employee information.

relational database A database that follows a group of mathematical rules proposed by E.F. Codd. A relational database consists of one or more tables. Each table has a single primary key. A relational database management system (RDBMS) stores and accesses the data as sets. The system catalog of the RDBMS is made up of tables, which are used to store information about the database and to ensure data integrity. An RDBMS also provides a data definition language (DDL), which is used to create tables and views. Data manipulation language (DML), user authorization, and transaction processing are also provided.

report The result of the use of database manipulation system. The result may be formatted by the user with the DBMS. A report may be displayed on a computer screen, printed out, or saved as a file.

REVOKE An SQL keyword that permits the owner of a database object to remove privileges previously granted to DBMS users. *See* GRANT.

row In a relation, or table, a row represents one occurrence, or record, of information about entities such as employees or departments. Each row is made up of values, one for each column in the table. Also known as a record.

Structured Query Language (SQL) A computer language developed by IBM to implement E.F. Codd's proposed rules for relational databases. It has since been adopted by many DBMSs. SQL is a standardized language, so data may be accessed across many different platforms, including personal computers, minicomputers, and mainframes. Another benefit of SQL is that software other than DBMSs, such as word processors and spreadsheets, can import data from SQL databases. SQL is "structured" because it follows rules. There are three kinds of commands in SQL. The first kind, data definition language commands, allow the creation of database objects such as tables and views. The second kind, data manipulation language commands, are used to retrieve information from the database, remove information from the database, and add information to it. Data control language commands grant and revoke privileges to access the database. Users can enter SQL commands interactively, or through an interface such as query by example (QBE).

system catalog A data dictionary consisting of descriptions of items in a database. The descriptions include the names of tables, the names of columns, and data types. The catalog also contains statistical information about the database. The catalog can be queried to find out about the structure and content of the database.

table *See* relation.

union An operation that combines two tables into a new table consisting of all of the rows of both tables.

view Virtual table that contains no data of its own, but the data are arranged like tables. A view contains all or part of a table or tables. Views can be used for security purposes, to allow others to see only portions of tables. They can also be used for convenience. A view can be defined as a complex query. The view itself can then be queried, eliminating the need to reenter the original query.

Index

+ (Addition operator), 9
/ (Division operator), 9
= (Equal to), 13
> (Greater than), 13
< (Less than), 13
* (Multiplication operator), 9
!+, ^=, <> (Not equal to), 13
- (Subtraction operator), 9

Addition. *See* **Calculations**
Aggregate functions, 25–52
AVG, 26, 86
COUNT(*), 32, 34
GROUP BY clause, 25–29
HAVING clause, 27–29
indexes, 31–32
subqueries involving, 85–89
summary tables, 28–31
Aggregation operations, 44
Aliases (table labels in joins), 80
ALL, 61–63, 74
ALTER TABLE . . . MODIFY statement, 152–53
ALTER TABLE statement, 5–6, 152–53
AND operator, 55, 57
ANY statement, 61–63
Arithmetic expressions. *See* Calculations
Asterisk (*), 5, 6
AUTOCOMMIT (ORACLE), 119–24
Automatic navigation, 3–4
AVG, 26, 86

BETWEEN operator, 54–55, 88, 110

Calculations, 9–24
expressions in ORDER BY clause, 14–15, 23, 24
expressions in WHERE clause, 13–14
operators, 9–13
percentage of total, 29–31
syntax for, 204
Cartesian product, 81
CATALOG table, 148, 180
Clause(s)
FROM, 5–6, 32, 80–81
GROUP BY, 25–29, 93
main purpose of, 44
sorting by, 45–46
HAVING, 27–29, 179
group selection using, 45
ORDER BY, 29, 34, 93, 95
expressions in, 14–15, 23, 24
SELECT, 5–6, 26–29, 79–81
calculation included in, 13
revised, 30
WHERE, 26–29, 80–81, 171–72, 179
arithmetic expressions in, 13–14
EXISTS and NOT EXISTS in, 66–67
predicates in, 53–67, 93
in subqueries, 92
COL table, 150
Column, in tables, 3
COLUMNS table, 149–50
Commands, syntax for, 201–5
See also specific statements and commands
COMMENT ON, 150–52
COMMIT, 118–19, 120–24
Complex queries, 53–57
hiding, 95
simplified data access and, 172–74
subqueries in. *See* Subqueries
with views, 172–74
Controls, transaction. *See* Transaction controls
Control tables, joins with, 89–91
Correlated references, 64–65
Correlated subqueries, 63–67
definition of, 64
table labels in, 64–65
COUNT(*), 26, 32, 34
CREATE INDEX statement, 31
CREATE TABLE statement, 5–6, 141–47, 163–64
data types in ORACLE, 143–44
naming rules, 142
as SELECT, 144–47
syntax, 141–42
CREATE VIEW syntax, 170, 178

Data definition language syntax, 204
Data dictionary, 147
Data security, 178–79

Data types, 34, 146–47
  specifying, 143
DELETE command, 95, 118–20, 174–77
DESCRIBE command, 146–47, 180–81
Dictionary, data, 147
Dictionary tables, 147–50
  CATALOG, 148, 180
  COL, 150
  COLUMNS, 149–50
  examine views with, 179–81
  TAB, 148–49
  VIEWS, 179–80
DISTINCT operator, 85, 113
Division. *See* Calculations

Embedded SELECT statement, 28
EXISTS, 66–67

FROM clause, 5–6, 32, 80–81
Functions, Aggregate. *See* Aggregate functions

GROUP BY clause, 25–29, 93
  main purpose of, 44
  sorting by, 45–46
Group function. *See* Aggregate functions
Groups, 25–28
  definition of, 25

HAVING clause, 27–29, 179
  group selection using, 45

Indexes, 31–32
IN operator, 54, 62
INSERT command, 28–29, 95, 119–20, 175, 178
  Format 2 of, 46

Joining tables, syntax for, 204
Joins, 79–115
  with control tables, 89–91
  definition of, 80
  outer join problem, 32–34, 51–52
  rules for, 108–9
  subqueries with, 91–92
  substituting for subqueries, 81–89
  table labels (aliases) in, 80
  with UNION, 92–95
  views with, 95–96, 173–74

LIKE predicate, 55
Logical condition (predicate), 27–28
Logical operators, 13–14, 53–54, 62–63
  rules of precedence, 55–56
Logical predicates, 53–54, 62–63

MAX, 26
MIN, 26
Multiplication. *See* Calculations

Navigation, automatic, 3–4
NOT EXISTS, 66–67
NOT IN predicate, 75
NOT operator, 55
NULL values, 29, 33, 57, 62, 143, 146–47, 153

Operator(s), 9–13
  AND, 55, 57
  BETWEEN, 54–55, 88, 110
  DISTINCT, 85, 113
  division (/), 9
  equal to (=), 13
  expressions with several, 10–13
  IN, 54, 62
  logical, 13–14, 53–54, 62–63
    rules of precedence, 55–56
  multiplication (*), 9
  NOT, 55
  OR, 55, 57
  rules of precedence, 11–13
  subtraction (-), 9
  value, 9–13
ORACLE, 143–47
  ALTER TABLE . . . MODIFY, 152–53
  AUTOCOMMIT, 119–24
  CREATE TABLE, 163–64
  CREATE TABLE . . . AS SELECT command, 144–46
  data types in, 143–44
  DESCRIBE command, 146–47, 180–81
  management transactions in, 117–24
  ORDER BY clause in, 14, 23, 24
  outer join problem solution in, 33, 51–52
ORDER BY clause, 29, 34, 93, 95
  expressions in, 14–15, 23, 24
OR operator, 55, 57
Outer join problem, 32–34, 51–52

Percentage of total calculation, 29–31
Pointers, 31
Predicates *See also* Operator(s)
  EXISTS, 66–67
  LIKE, 55
  NOT EXISTS, 66–67
  NOT IN, 75
  subqueries in multiple, 59–61
  in WHERE clause, 53–67, 93
    in subqueries, 92

Queries
  complex, 53–57
    hiding, 95
    simplified data access and, 172–74
    subqueries in. *See* Subqueries
    with views, 172–74
  definition of, 6

Read-only views, 95–96, 175
References, correlated, 64–65
Relational database, 2–4
  definition of, 2
REMARKS column, 150–51
ROLLBACK, 120–24
Row, in tables, 3

Security, data, 178–79
SELECT statement(s), 5–6
  embedded, 28
  FROM clause in, 5–6, 32, 80–81

SELECT statements(s) (*cont'd*)
SELECT clause in, 5–6, 26–29, 79–81
calculation included in, 13
revised, 30
syntax for, 201
UNION operation on, 34, 92–93
Semicolon, as statement terminator, 7
Sorting, with GROUP BY, 45–46
Structured Query Language (SQL), 1–7
automatic navigation, 3–4
basic concepts of, 2–3
definition of, 1
practical advantages of, 3–4
Subqueries, 57–78
ANY and ALL in, 61–63
correlated, 63–67
definition of, 64
table labels in, 64–65
definition of, 58
EXISTS and NOT EXISTS, 66–67
IN operator with, 62
involving aggregate functions, 85–89
joins with, 91–92
rules for using, 59–63
in multiple predicates, 59–61
substituting joins for, 81–89
syntax for, 203
Sub-SELECT, 28–29
Subtraction. *See* Calculations
SUM, 26
Summary tables, 28–31
Syntax for commands, 201–5

Table labels (correlation names)
in correlated subqueries, 64–65
in joins (aliases), 80
Tables, 2–3, 141–68
ALTER TABLE, 5–6, 152–53
COMMENT ON, 150–52
control, 89–91
CREATE TABLE, 5–6, 141–47, 163–64
data types in ORACLE, 143–44
naming rules, 142
as SELECT, 144–47
syntax, 141–42
definition of, 141
DESCRIBE command (ORACLE), 144–47
dictionary, 147–50
CATALOG, 148, 180
COL, 150
COLUMNS, 149–50
examine views with, 179–81
TAB, 148–49
VIEWS, 179–80
joining, syntax, 204
retrieving entire, 6–7
rows and columns in, 3
sample, 4–5
summary, 28–31
values in, 3
TAB table, 148–49
Transaction, definition of, 117
Transaction controls, 117–40
AUTOCOMMIT (ORACLE), 119–24
COMMIT, 118–19, 120–24
definition of, 118
ROLLBACK, 120–24

Underscore symbol (_), 55
UNION operation, 29, 33–34, 92–95
on SELECT statement, 34, 92–93
UNIQUE INDEX, 31
UPDATE command, 95, 118–19, 175, 177–78

Value(s)
NULL, 29, 33, 57, 62, 143, 146–47, 153
in tables, 3
Value operators, 9–13
precedence of, 11–13
Views, 169–97
complex queries, 172–74
CREATE VIEW syntax, 170, 178
data access, simplified, 172–74
data security, 178–79
definition of, 169
DELETE command, 174–77
dictionary tables, 179–81
dropping from database, 179
INSERT command, 175, 178
joins with, 95–96, 173–74
modifying data through, 174–78
purpose of, 169–70
read-only, 95–96, 175
UPDATE command, 95, 118–19, 175, 177–78
VIEWS table, 179–80

WHERE clause, 26–29, 80–81, 171–72, 179
arithmetic expressions in, 13–14
EXISTS in, 66–67
NOT EXISTS in, 66–67
predicates in, 53–67, 93
BETWEEN, 54–55
IN, 54
LIKE, 55
in subqueries, 92
Wildcard, 55
WITH CHECK OPTION, 178

IBM® PC DISKS to Accompany LEARNING ADVANCED SQL

Prentice Hall

YOU SHOULD CAREFULLY READ THE FOLLOWING TERMS AND CONDITIONS BEFORE OPENING THIS DISKETTE PACKAGE. OPENING THIS DISKETTE PACKAGE INDICATES YOUR ACCEPTANCE OF THESE TERMS AND CONDITIONS. IF YOU DO NOT AGREE WITH THEM, YOU SHOULD PROMPTLY RETURN THE PACKAGE UNOPENED, AND YOUR MONEY WILL BE REFUNDED.

Prentice Hall, Inc. provides this program and licenses its use. You assume reponsibility for the selection of the program to achieve your intended results, and for the installation, use, and results obtained from the program. This license extends only to use of the program in the United States or countries in which the program is marketed by duly authorized distributors.

LICENSE

You may:

a. use the program;

b. copy the program into any machine-readable form without limit;

c. modify the program and/or merge it into another program in support of your use of the program.

LIMITED WARRANTY

THE PROGRAM IS PROVIDED "AS IS" WITHOUT WARRANTY OF ANY KIND, EITHER EXPRESSED OR IMPLIED, INCLUDING, BUT NOT LIMITED TO, THE IMPLIED WARRANTIES OF MERCHANTABILITY AND FITNESS FOR A PARTICULAR PURPOSE. THE ENTIRE RISK AS TO THE QUALITY AND PERFORMANCE OF THE PROGRAM IS WITH YOU. SHOULD THE PROGRAM PROVE DEFECTIVE, YOU (AND NOT PRENTICE HALL, INC. OR ANY AUTHORIZED DISTRIBUTOR) ASSUME THE ENTIRE COST OF ALL NECESSARY SERVICING, REPAIR, OR CORRECTION.

SOME STATES DO NOT ALLOW THE EXCLUSION OF IMPLIED WARRANTIES, SO THE ABOVE EXCLUSION MAY NOT APPLY TO YOU. THIS WARRANTY GIVES YOU SPECIFIC LEGAL RIGHTS AND YOU MAY ALSO HAVE OTHER RIGHTS THAT VARY FROM STATE TO STATE.

Prentice Hall, Inc. does not warrant that the functions contained in the program will meet your requirements or that the operation of the program will be uninterrupted or error free.

However, Prentice Hall, Inc., warrants the diskette(s) on which the program is furnished to be free from defects in materials and workmanship under normal use for a period of ninety (90) days from the date of delivery to you as evidenced by a copy of your receipt.

LIMITATIONS OF REMEDIES

Prentice Hall's entire liability and your exclusive remedy shall be:

1. the replacement of any diskette not meeting Prentice Hall's "Limited Warranty" and that is returned to Prentice Hall with a copy of your purchase order, or
2. if Prentice Hall is unable to deliver a replacement diskette or cassette that is free of defects in materials or workmanship, you may terminate this Agreement by returning the program, and your money will be refunded.

IN NO EVENT WILL PRENTICE HALL BE LIABLE TO YOU FOR ANY DAMAGES, INCLUDING ANY LOST PROFITS, LOST SAVINGS, OR OTHER INCIDENTAL OR CONSEQUENTIAL DAMAGES ARISING OUT OF THE USE OR INABILITY TO USE SUCH PROGRAM EVEN IF PRENTICE HALL OR AN AUTHORIZED DISTRIBUTOR HAS BEEN ADVISED OF THE POSSIBILITY OF SUCH DAMAGES, OR FOR ANY CLAIM BY ANY OTHER PARTY.

SOME STATES DO NOT ALLOW THE LIMITATION OR EXCLUSION OF LIABILITY FOR INCIDENTAL OR CONSEQUENTIAL DAMAGES, SO THE ABOVE LIMITATION OR EXCLUSION MAY NOT APPLY TO YOU.

GENERAL

You may not sublicense, assign, or transfer the license or the program except as expressly provided in this Agreement. Any attempt otherwise to sublicense, assign, or transfer any of the rights, duties, or obligations hereunder is void.

This Agreement will be governed by the laws of the State of New York.

Should you have any questions concerning this Agreement, you may contact Prentice Hall, Inc., by writing to:

Prentice Hall
College Division
Englewood Cliffs, N.J. 07632

Should you have any questions concerning technical support you may write to:

Wellesley Software
376 Boylston Street
Boston, MA 02116

YOU ACKNOWLEDGE THAT YOU HAVE READ THIS AGREEMENT, UNDERSTAND IT, AND AGREE TO BE BOUND BY ITS TERMS AND CONDITIONS. YOU FURTHER AGREE THAT IT IS THE COMPLETE AND EXCLUSIVE STATEMENT OF THE AGREEMENT BETWEEN US THAT SUPERSEDES ANY PROPOSAL OR PRIOR AGREEMENT, ORAL OR WRITTEN, AND ANY OTHER COMMUNICATIONS BETWEEN US RELATING TO THE SUBJECT MATTER OF THIS AGREEMENT.

ISBN-0-13-528712-X